THE REPUBLIC OF KARAKALPA

РЕСПУБЛИКА КАРАКАЛПАКСТАН

Government: Autonomous republic of Uzbekistan	**Правительство:** Республика Каракалпакстан - республика в составе Узбекистана.
Administrative capital: Nukus	**Столица:** Нукус
Official languages: Karakalpak, Uzbek	**Официальные языки:** Каракалпакский, узбекский
Territory: 166,600 square km	**Территория:** 166,6 тыс. кв. км.
Population: 1,639,000	**Население:** 1,639 миллиона человек
Religion: Islam	**Религия:** Ислам (Сунниты)
Time zone: UTC +5	**Часовой пояс:** UTC+5
Internet TLD: .uz	**Интернет:** .uz
Country calling code: +998	**Вызывающий код страны:** +998

Dear traveler,

I am delighted that you hold in your hands the first guidebook of Karakalpakstan and I would like to invite you to discover this remote but very impressive region in the North-Western part of Uzbekistan.

Karakalpakstan has its touristic potential off the much-frequented tracks of the Silk Road: ruins of pre-Islamic civilization in South Karakalpakstan, stunning art works of banned Soviet artists in the Savitsky collection in Nukus and the today's visible environmental consequences in Muynak caused by the retreat of the Aral Sea.

Since 2005, Deutsche Gesellschaft für Internationale Zusammenarbeit (GIZ) promotes the economic development in selected regions of Uzbekistan. In Karakalpakstan, we are amongst others supporting the tourism sector. Currently a GIZ expert works in cooperation with touristic institutions on site, aiming at developing the regions' potentials in the field of tourism.

Hence, I acknowledge with pleasure the professionalization of the tourism sector in Karakalpakstan during the last years.

I am sure you will experience and enjoy the extraordinary hospitality of Karakalpak people. This guidebook may help you to discover the numerous breathtaking attractions of Karakalpakstan.

Carl F. Taestensen
Country Director of GIZ Uzbekistan

Дорогой путешественник !

Я рад, что вы держите в руках первый путеводитель по Каракалпакстану и я хотел бы пригласить Вас открыть для себя этот отдаленный, но очень впечатляющий регион в северо-западной части Узбекистана.

Каракалпакстан имеет свой туристический потенциал среди частопосещаемых маршрутов Великого шелкового пути: руины доисламской цивилизации в Южном Каракалпакстане, потрясающие произведения искусства запрещенных советских художников в коллекции И.В.Савицкого в Нукусе и видимые экологические последствия в Муйнаке, вызванных усыханием Аральского моря.

С 2005 года Германское Общество по международному сотрудничеству (GIZ) поддерживает экономическое развитие в избранных регионах Узбекистана. В Каракалпакстане, мы среди прочих проектов также поддерживаем сектор туризма. В настоящее время эксперт GIZ работает в сотрудничестве с туристическими учреждениями на местах, направленных на развитие потенциала регионов в сфере туризма. Следовательно , я с удовольствием признаю профессионализация сектора туризма в Каракалпакстане в последние годы.

Я уверен, вы будете испытывать и наслаждаться чрезвычайно высоким гостеприимством каракалпакского народа. Этот путеводитель поможет вам открыть для себя многочисленные захватывающие дух достопримечательности Каракалпакстана.

Карл Ф. Тестенсен
Страновой директор GIZ Узбекистан

KARAKALPAKSTAN – CHARM OF A DESERT LANDSCAPE

КАРАКАЛПАКСТАН – ОЧАРОВАНИЕ ПУСТЫННОГО ПЕЙЗАЖА

Mukhabbat Kamalova

Мухаббат Камалова

Hearty nomad hospitality, vast desert, remnants of the ancient and recent past: there are many ways to describe Karakalpakstan. The region is known around the world for the ecological disaster of the shrinking Aral Sea, for the astonishing views of ships stranded on land miles and miles from any water - but has so much more to offer visitors.

The 'country of the black hats' is the literal translation of Karakalpakstan, with the Karakalpaks a people sharing characteristics with all Turkic populations of Central Asia. With the Uzbeks, they share a tradition of communal living; with the Kazakhs, a common language; with the Kyrgyz, the hats, white for the Kyrgyz, and black for the Karakalpaks; with the Turkmen, traditional embroidery.

Сердечное гостеприимство кочевого народа, обширные пустыни, остатки древнего и недавнего прошлого: есть много способов описать Каракалпакстан. Этот регион известен по всему миру как регион экологической катастрофы из-за высыхания Аральского моря, с изумительным видом на корабли, выброшенными на берег на тысячи милей от воды - регион, который может предложить посетителям много интересного.

«Страна черных шапок» дословный перевод слова Каракалпакстан. Каракалпаки народ, имеющий схожесть со всеми тюркоязычными народами в Центральной Азии. С узбеками их связывают общие традиции совместного проживания, с казахами – общий язык, с киргизами шапки (у киргизов белые шапки, у каракалпаков – черные); с туркменами –традиционная вышивка. Что менее известно о Каракал-

What is less known about Karakalpakstan is that besides the vast desert, the region offers considerable variety: city lights appear in the desert night; a well-developed system of lakes is home to a variety of birds; the spectacular Ustyurt Plateau, thought to separate the landmasses of Asia and Europe, resembles Hollywood's vision of a Mars landscape, an otherworldly stillness amid the natural world.

This guidebook offers you a closer look at Karakalpakstan, its history and modernity, the Aral Sea, flora and fauna as well as its culture, traditions and customs. Welcome to somewhere truly remarkable.

пакстане, кроме обширной пустыни , регион предлагает множество разнообразий: ночная пустыня с вдруг возникающими огнями города; развитая система озер с богатым разнообразием птиц; впечатляющее плато Устюрт, разделяющее континенты Азии и Европы, таинственная тишина окружающего мира.

Путеводитель предлагает вам поближе познакомиться с Каракалпакстаном, его историю и современность, с Аральским морем, флорой и фауной, а также культурой, траидиями и обычаями народа.

Добро пожаловать в мир настоящего.

A BRIEF HISTORY OF KARAKALPAKSTAN

КРАТКАЯ ИСТОРИЯ КАРАКАЛПАКСТАНА

Karakalpakstan is an autonomous region of the Republic of Uzbekistan, with its centre in the city of Nukus. It has its own constitution, flag and anthem, but local laws refer to Uzbek national law.

The population is estimated to be up two million people, chiefly made up of Karakalpaks, Uzbeks and Kazakhs, along with minorities of Russians, Tartars and Turkmen among others. Although most of Karakalpakstan is desert, canals lead off from the Amu Darya River, known historically as the Oxus, for agriculture: cotton is the main crop.

The earliest settlers lived beside the Amu Darya: hunters and fishermen from Paleolithic and Neolithic times, from 6,000 BC up until when fortifications appeared, approximately 2,500 years ago. Then, the region, known as Khorezm, was a satellite of the Persian Empire, before gaining

Каракалпакстан является суверенной Республикой в составе Республики Узбекистан, со столицей в городе Нукус. Республика Каракалпакстан имеет собственную конституцию, флаг и гимн, и местное законодательство не противоречит узбекскому национальному законодательству.

Население Республики составляет около 2 миллионов человек, в основном проживают каракалпаки, узбеки и казахи, среди других народов меньшинств проживают русские, татары, туркмены и др. Несмотря на то, что огромную часть Каракалпакстана занимает пустыня, от реки Амударья, исторически известная как Окс, отходят каналы для орошения, основной сельскохозяйственной культурой является хлопок.

Первые поселенцы жили у Амударьи: охотники и рыбаки из периода палеолита и неолита, с 6000 г. до н.э. до военных укреплений, кото-

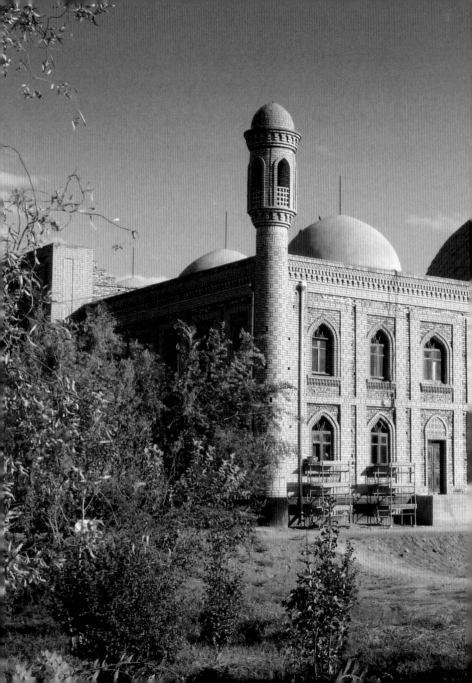

independence in the succeeding centuries.

What marks the region out from other parts of southern Central Asia, including Afghanistan, is the absence of the Hellenistic influence. Alexander the Great did not attempt to seize the region, and continued marching onwards to India, leaving it to prosper while his posthumous empire underwent internal discord.

Meanwhile, Central Asia was gradually assuming its place in world history as the trade highway between China and Rome, otherwise known as the Silk Road. This continued despite repeated incursions by the Huns, in the 4th century; the Turks in the 6th century; the Arabs in the 8th century, which saw the advent of what is now a chiefly Sunni Islam; and by the 13th century the most destructive of all – the Mongols, under Genghis Khan. Cities were razed to the ground, whole populations massacred; agriculture was devastated, and canal systems broken, allowing the desert to regain sovereignty of enormous tracts of land. However, the Silk Road was too important to be allowed to disintegrate, and lands west of the Amu Darya recovered to allow trade.

Yet, Tamerlane, another renowned conqueror of Central Asia, kept

рые появились около 2500 лет назад. Затем, регион, известный как Хорезм, был сторонником Персидской империи, до обретения независимости в последующие века.

Что отличает регион от других частей юга Центральной Азии, включая Афганистан, это отсутствие эллинистического влияния. Александр Великий не пытался захватить регион , а продолжал дальше идти в Индию, оставив ее процветать, а его посмертная империя претерпела внутренние разногласия.

Между тем, Центральная Азия постепенно берет свое место в мировой истории, как торговая магистраль между Китаем и Римом, по другому известная как Шелковый путь. Эта ситуация продолжалась, несмотря на неоднократные вторжения гуннов в 4 веке, турков в 6-ом веке, арабов в 8-м веке, которые видели рождение ислама суннитского направления, и монголов под предводительством Чингизхана в 13-м веке, которые разрушили все. Города были разрушены до основания, уничтожено все население, сельское хозяйство было разорено, и системы каналов нарушены , позволяющие пустыне иметь свой суверенитет . Тем не менее, Шелковый путь был слишком важен, чтобы разорить его, и земли к западу от Амударьи были восстановлены для торговли.

the people in suspense with his campaigns in the late 14th century. It wasn't until almost 400 years ago that the old canal network began to stir into life again, in parts. This was developed considerably by the Soviet Union during the 20th century, as irrigation for Uzbekistan as an agricultural hub, and which ultimately led to the shrinking of the Aral Sea as canals fed off the Amu Darya which had historically fed the great inland water mass.

Initially, the Karakalpak Autonomous Region was designated within Kazakhstan in 1924, then eight years later within Russia, before finally being added to Uzbekistan in 1936.

В конце 14 века наступил период правления знаменитого Тамерлана. Это было до почти 400 лет назад, что старые сети канала частями начали движение . Значительное развитие оно получило в Советском Союзе в 20-м веке, когда большое внимание было уделено ирригации в Узбекистане, и воды Аральского моря отводились к каналам, что в конечном итоге привело к высыханиюм Аральского моря.

Первоначально Каракалпакская автономная область входила в состав Казахстана в 1924 году, спустя восемь лет в состав России, пока, наконец, в 1936 году начала входить с состав Республики Узбекистан.

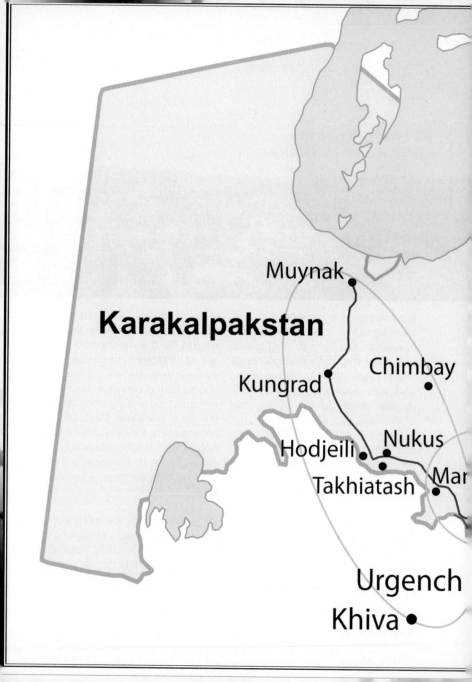

Muynak

Karakalpakstan

Chimbay

Kungrad

Nukus

Hodjeili

Takhiatash

Mar

Urgench

Khiva

Map of Uzbekistan

khtakupir

eruni

Turtkul

Map
of Karakalpakstan

TRACKS OF ANCIENT CIVILIZATION
СЛЕДЫ ДРЕВНЕЙ ЦИВИЛИЗАЦИИ

During the prosperous time of ancient Khorezm, in what now makes up much of the Karakalpakstan region, settlements and even cities developed along the former river bed of the Amu Darya, and fortified citadels and frontier fortresses were built on the boundaries of settled land. Due to a later change of direction in the Amu Darya, the population followed the water, abandoned their settlements and cities and left them to time and to the sand. This explains why today these witnesses of pre-Islamic times can only be found in the vast desert, some several kilometres away from main roads and difficult to access.

Excavations during the famous Khorezm Archeological and Ethnographic Expedition (1945 - 1950) led by the Russian scientist Sergei P. Tolstov (1907 - 1976) revealed the historic wealth of the ancient kalas (forts) and the high level of cultural development during Khorezmian times.

В процветающее время древние поселения Хорезма и развитые города располагались вдоль бывшего русла реки Амударьи, укрепленные пограничные крепости строились на границах оседлой земли. Впоследствии с изменением русла реки Амударьи, население направилось за течением воды, отказавшись от своих обжитых поселков и городов, и оставили их времени и песку. Это объясняет, почему сегодня эти свидетельства истории доисламского времени найдены только в огромной пустыне, в нескольких километрах от основной дороги и частично труднодоступны.

Раскопки в период знаменитой Хорезмской археолого - этнографической экспедиции под руководством русского ученого С.П. Толстова (1907-1976) показали историческое богатство древних городищ и высокий уровень культурного развития Хо-

Around 40 ruins of those ancient fortresses are located on the territory of Karakalpakstan. Some worth seeing ruins can be found in the district of Elli Kala (meaning 'fifty castles' in Karakalpak) close to the city of Bustan. Among them are Ayaz Kala, Toprak Kala and Kizil Kala. Although they can easily approached by car, it is not without difficulties to enter them on the steep sandy footpaths. Other impressive kalas, such as Djanbas Kala and Dzhanpik Kala, are easy to enter, but are located quite far away from tarred roads.

The spectacular settlement of Ayaz Kala is located 23 km northeast of the city Bustan along a small tarred road, and is actually a complex of three monuments of different eras which were mainly garrisons for the defense forces. The fortress Ayaz Kala I on the top of the hill dates back from 300 - 400 BCE. The walls are well preserved and today it is still possible to identify a corridor of 2.5 m wide between the outer and inner walls, and double storey gallery with loopholes for archers. The entrance to the fortress was in the south wall and was well protected by a rectangular building with a passage into the east wall. From this side you have an excellent view to the south over Ayaz Kala II. This oval fort dates back to the 7th century, and in the

резмского периода. На территории современного Каракалпакстана находятся около 40 древних городищ. Некоторые важные из этих древних руин можно найти в районе Элликкала («50 замков» на каракалпакском языке) на юге Каракалпакстана, недалеко от города Бустан. Среди них: Аяз-кала, Топрак-кала, Кизыл-кала. К ним можно легко приехать на машине, и без трудностей забраться по крутой песчаной тропинке. В другие впечатляющие городища как Джанбас кала и Джанпык кала также можно легко забраться, но они расположены достаточно далеко асфальтированных дорог.

Захватывающее поселение Аяз-кала находится в 23 км от северу-востока города Бустан, вдоль небольшой асфальтированной дороги, оно является комплексом из трех памятников из разных эпох, служившим гарнизоном для обороны. Крепость Аяз-кала I расположена на самой вершине холма и датирована IV-III вв до н. э. Стены хорошо сохранились и сегодня можно рассмотреть коридор шириной 2,5 м между наружные и внутренние стены - двухъярусные галереи для лучников и бойницы. Въезд находился в южной стене крепости и зашишен предвратным прямоугольным соору-

13th century this castle was partly used for housing. Below the two fortresses, located in the open plain, the ruins of the largest of the three fortresses, Ayaz Kala III, can be recognized. On the top of the plateau the Ayaz-Kala Yurt Camps will welcome its visitors within the 12 cosy yurts.

The ruins of the fortress Toprak Kala are located 12 km northwest of Bustan, close to the main road from Turtkul to Nukus. The construction of the city dates back to the 2nd century, and it was the location of the residence of the ruler of the state, confirmed by skin-written records. The complex of Toprak Kala consisted of a housing settlement all along the straight street inside the fort; a high-lying palace; a fire temple; and an external palace complex in the north. The main street led from the gate on the south wall to the north. Perpendicular lanes divided the buildings into several blocks. Most of them had been living houses.

Much of the high-lying palace was occupied by ceremonial rooms and a sanctuary; a fire altar indicates that the residents were Zoroastrians. The walls were decorated with paintings, and in five halls there were clay bas-relief with multicolored paintings. In the beginning of the 4th century Toprak Kala lost its importance after

жением с проходом в восточной стене. С этой стороны у вас есть отличный вид на юг Аяз-Калы II. Этот форт овальной формы, датируется VII-VIII веке н. э. В XIII веке крепость частично используется под жилье. Ниже эти крепости, расположенное но открытой равнине является самой крупной из этих трех сооружение, руин Аяз-кала III. На вершине плато вас будет приветствовать юртовый лагерь, состоящий из уютных 12 юрт.

Руины крепости Топрак-Кала расположены в 12 км от запада города Бустон и находится в непосредственной близости от главной дороги из Турткуль в Нукус. Строительство города датировано II-III веками н. э.. Здесь находилась резиденция правителя государства, согласно найденным письменным памятникам на коже. В состав комплекса Топрак-кала входят: городище, возведенное вдоль прямой улицы внутри крепости, высокий дворец, храм огня и внешний северный комплекс. От ворот с юга на север шла центральная улица. Перпендикулярные ей переулки делили застройку на несколько кварталов. Большинство из них были жилыми.

Большую часть высокого дворца занимал комплекс парадных

the construction of a new palace in the fortress of Fir Kala by the new ruler Afrigom. During the 7th century the fort became ruined.

Kizil Kala, the red fortress, is one of the best preserved fortresses in Karakalpakstan and is about 2 km to the west of Toprak Kala. The fortress was originally built in the 1st – 4th centuries CE, then abandoned and reconstructed in the 12th and 13th century.

The well-preserved walls stand in the middle of fields and have an almost square form, measuring 65 m by 63 m. As a defensive fortress, Kizil Kala was also part of a chain of Khorezmian fortifications built by the government to protect the north-eastern boundary of the region. At the same time the fortress was the center of the regional agricultural economy and the junction of caravan routes across the Sultanuizdag chain.

Great Guldursun, the largest fortress of old Khorezm, is located 26 km north east of Turtkul just beside the road. It was one of the great border fortresses of Khorezm. The outer walls and towers date to the 12th century. The discovery of token coins on the archeological site revealed the fact that the fortress was inhabited at least until 1220, when Muhammad, the Shah

помещений и святилищ, алтарь огня указывает, что жители были зароострийцами. Стены были украшены росписями, а в пяти залах - глиняными барельефами с полихромной раскраской.

После строительства новым правителем Афригом нового дворца в крепости Фир-кала в начале IV века, Топрак-кала теряет свое значение. Полное опустошение происходит к VII веку.

Кызыл кала, красная крепость одним из наиболее сохранившихся городов и находится примерно в 2 км от запада комплекса Топрак-кала. Крепость была построена в I-IV вв. нашей эры, затем в XII-XIII вв была реконструирована. Хорошо сохранившиеся стены стоят посреди полей и имеют почти квадратную форму размерами 65 x 63 м. Была возведена, вероятно, как оборонительная крепость и входила в цепь хорезмийских укреплений, созданных государством для защиты северо-восточного рубежа античного Хорезма. Одновременно крепость была центром сельскохозяйственной округи и узлом караванных дорог через горный хребет Султануиздаг.

Большой Гульдурсун - одна из крупных пограничных крепостей

of Khorezm, ruled, and when the Mongols invaded.

As always for ancient settlements, there are legends and stories surrounding the origin of its name. According to legend, for a long time the Mongols could not conquer the city and laid siege to it. The city's residents, already starved, decided to use a trick: they fed a bull with wheat and grains and released it outside. The Mongols, starving as well, caught the bull, slaughtered it and found the bull's stomach full of cereals. And they thought: "If the bulls are fed with wheat, then we will need to wait a long time until the people are hungry enough to surrender." They were about to abandon the siege and depart when Guldursun, the daughter of the city's ruler and who had fallen in love with one of the Mongol leaders, sent a message to the Mongols explained the bull was a trick, and asking the besiegers to hold out a little longer, so that the people would finally be forced to open the gates and surrender. And so it happened. The Mongols however did not honour Guldursun, but caught and executed her, saying that she who had betrayed her own people would also betray them.

Djanbas Kala - the imposing frontier fortress lies in the north of the city Turtkul. It was built in the 4th century

Хорезма, расположена в 26 км от северо-востока Турткуля, рядом с дорогой. Внешние стены и башни датируются XII веком н.э. Судя по находкам монет, можно определить, что последний период обживания памятника относится к 1220 году, к моменту правления Мухаммеда Хорезмшаха, т.е. ко времени нашествия Монгольских войск в Хорезм. Об этом же свидетельствует легенда: монголы не могли взять город и долгое время держали его в осаде. Жители города, которые уже голодали, решили применить трюк и накормили быка пшеницей и другими злаками и выпустили наружу. Монголы, поймав этого быка зарезали и увидели, что желудок быка полон злаками. Тогда они подумали: «если быков кормят пшеницей, то нужно долго ждать, пока народ проголодается» и хотели снять осаду. Но дочь местного правителя по имени Гулдурсун, увидев одного из монгольских полководцев, влюбилляется в него. Тогда Гулдурсун отправляет монголам сообщение, что это хитрость жителей города. На самом деле они живут впроголодь. Если монголы немного потерпят, то жители вынуждены будут открыть ворота. Так и вышло. А монголы не учли поступок Гулдурсун, её поймали и казнили, сказав, что тот,

BCE and differs from most Khorezm fortresses due to the lack of towers in the walls and corners. The double walls of the fortress and maze are well preserved with a height of up to 20 m. The outer wall is completely covered with the narrow and high arrow-shaped loopholes arranged in a checkerboard pattern. Djanbas Kala is very worthwhile visiting. In a small distance a Yurt camp has been installed to welcome and serve visitors.

Along the road to Nukus, 12 km behind the turnoff to the Badai-Tugai Nature Reserve, a side road on the left leads to Dzhanpik Kala. Located at the banks of the Amu Darya River this is the most picturesque of the Khorezm fortresses. Its foundations date back to the 4th - 1st BCE, the walls visible today were built in the 9th and 10th centuries CE. A citadel, in a rectangular shape, is still remaining in the eastern part. During excavation works numerous findings were revealed, earlier brought from east and west including China, Egypt, Russia, Europe, and India. The city served as a port in medieval times. Nearby the fortress Gyaur Kala is also to be found.

A circular boulder, Chilpik, possibly the regional symbol of Karakalpakstan, rises to the sky and is visible from afar. It is located about 45 km to the south of Nukus.

кто предал свой народ, предаст и их.

Джанбас-кала, внушительная пограничная крепость находится на севере города Турткуль. Она была построена в IV веке до н.э. и отличается от большинства крепостей Хорезма отсутствием башен на стенах и углах. Двойные стены крепости и лабиринт хорошо сохранились на высоте до 20 м. Внешняя стена вся сплошь покрыта узкими и высокими стреловидными бойницами, расположенных в шахматном порядке. Джанбас кала стоит посмотреть. Недалеко можно навестить маленький юртовый лагерь.

Вдоль дороги в Нукус 12 км после поворота на Бадай-Тугайский заповедник, боковая дорога ведёт влево в укрепление Джанпык-кала. Расположенная на берегу реки Амударья, она является самой живописной из Хорезмийских крепостей. Его основы восходят к IV – I вв. до нашей эры, стены которые мы видим сегодня датируются IX-X вв нашей эры. В восточной части сохранилась цитадель в виде прямоугольника паховых стен. При раскопках обнаружены многочисленные находки ранее привезенные из различных стран Востока и Запада. (Китая, Егип-

Originally constructed in the 1st century CE the building served as a dakhma or a Tower of Silence, and was used by Zoroastrians to place their dead under the open sky, to be devoured by birds. Once the bones were picked cleaned, the family would gather them and place them in an ossuary (a clay or stone urn) for burial. The surrounding hills of Chilpik are filled with graves, and samples of such burial ossuaries can be visited in the museum in Nukus.

The spectacular complex of Mizdakh-khan is worth a visit. It is located close to the city Khodjeli, about 25 – 30 km west of Nukus. Mizdakh-khan is an impressive site whose various monuments are sited on and between three small hills. The ruins which are spread out between the citadel and necropolis once were one of the cities of the Golden Horde of Khorezm, which was located for more than 2,000 years on international trade routes. This ancient city of Mizdakh-khan dates to 4th century BCE. Some parts of the impressive necropolis are today still used by the local population as a cemetery. The oldest graves date back to 2nd century BCE, and demonstrate the burial techniques of Zoroastrianism, such as the use of ossuaries.

Among the worth seeing monuments there is the well known

та, России, Европы, Индии). Городище служило портовым городом в средневековье. Недалеко находится крепость Гяур-кала Султанууиздагская.

Круглая каменная глыба, символ Каракалпакстана, высится повсюду видимый в небо. **Чилпык** находится 45 км от юга города Нукус. Построенный в первом веке нашей эры, этот археологический памятник служил дахмой или башней молчания, и был использован зароострийцами для выставления тел умерших под открытым небом, на съедение птицам. После того, как кости очищались от плоти, семья умершего собирала их и помещала в глиняные или каменные урны для погребения. Окружающие Чилпык холмы заполнены могилами, и образцы таких погребальных урн можно увидеть в музее в Нукусе.

Впечатляющий комплекс Миздахан стоит посетить. Он расположен недалеко от города Ходжейли, примерно от 25-30 к западу от Нукуса. Миздакхан является впечатляющим местом с различными памятниками, расположенными на трех небольших холмах. Руины, разбросанные между цитаделью и некрополь, когда-то были одним из городов Золото-ордынского Хорезма, находив-

mausoleum of Mazlumkhan-Sulu, which dates back to the 14th century. It was constructed underground, only its cupola is visible above the ground. There are three unknown tombs inside the mausoleum and a lot of legends about this place. Other monuments at the site are the 25 m long sarcophagus of the giant Shamun Nabi, which is still considered a sacred place, as well as the holy place of Djumarat Khasab, which may have once been used as dakhma. Women with difficulties in bearing children still come here to roll down the hill to be cured. The ruins of the citadel Gyaur Kala are located on a third hill to the south west.

Overnight in yurt camps close to the Kalas:

Ayaz-Kala Yurt Camp
Prices/person: 50 USD, including meals (dinner, breakfast, lunch)
☎ +998-61-350 59 09,
+998-94-644-86-99
(Rano, in the camp)
@ ayazkala_tur@mail.ru

Djanbas-Kala Yurt Camp
Prices/person: 25 USD, including breakfast/ 35 USD, including dinner, breakfast
☎ +998-93-201-00-00,
+998-90-719-08-70
(Dilshod speaks English)
@ Djanbaskala@mail.ru

шийся вот уже более 2000 лет на путях международной торговли. Этот древний город Миздакхан датируется IV-веком до н.э. Комплекс сейчас расположен в нескольких холмах, некоторые из которых сегодня используется местным населением в качестве мазара (кладбища). Самые старые могилы датируются II веком до н.э., и указывают на особенности погребального культа зороастризма, таких как использование оссуариев.

Среди памятников стоит посмотреть известный Мавзолей Мазлумхан-сулу, восходящий к XIV веку. Памятник отличается своей архитектурой – над землей виден только купол. Также внутри мавзолея находятся три неизвестные гробницы и существует множество легенд об этом памятнике. Другим памятником является саркофаг гигантского Шамун Наби, длиной в 25 м, который до сих пор является священном местом, также как считается священным местом холм Джумарт Хассап, которая используется в качестве дахмы. Женщины, не имеющие возможность родить детей, приезжают сюда, чтобы скатиться по склону холма, в надежде вымолить ребенка. Руины цитадели Гяур кала, расположены на третьем холме на юго-западной стороне.

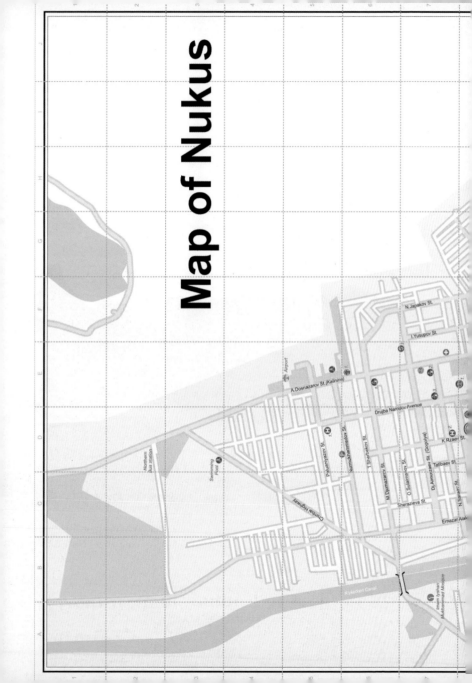

Map of Nukus

Northern Bus station

Swimming Pool

Chimbai Highway

A. Dosnazarov St. (Kalinine)

Airport

N. Japakov St.

I. Yusupov St.

Druba Narodov Avenue

Pakumyazov St.

Numukhammadov St.

I. Shchekov St.

M. Dyumazarov St.

O. Sulaimanov St.

Dj. Aimurzaev St. (Gogolya)

K. Rzaev St.

Tatibaev St.

Sherazieva St.

N. Staev St.

Emazar Alak.

Kijkobran Canal

Imam Syshan.
Mukhammad Mosque

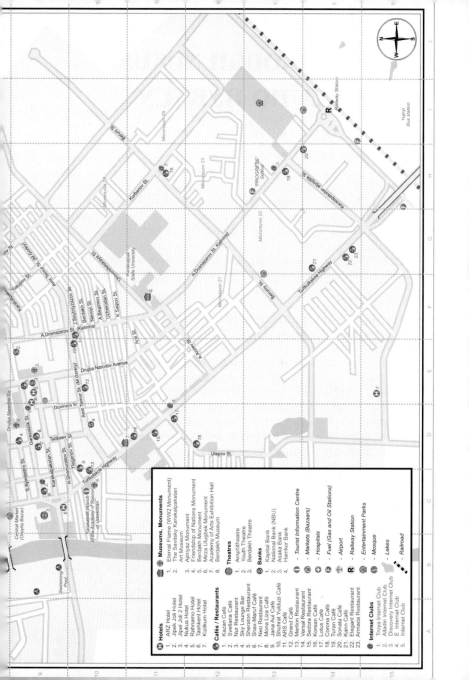

Hotels
1. ARZ Hotel
2. Jipek Joli Hotel
3. Jipek Joli 2 Hotel
4. Nukus Hotel
5. Rahnamo Hotel
6. Tashkent Hotel
7. Kizilkum Hotel

Cafés / Restaurants
1. Kazan Café
2. Svetlana Café
3. Nur Restaurant
4. Sky Lounge Bar
5. Sheraton Restaurant
6. Shax-Manuf Café
7. Neo Restaurant
8. Mona Liza Café
9. Jana Aul Café
10. Shuhrat Yulduzi Café
11. ARS Café
12. Grand Café
13. Merlion Restaurant
14. Versal Restaurant
15. Sedora Restaurant
16. Korean Café
17. Lotus Café
18. Corona Café
19. Turan Café
20. Sonata Café
21. Kann Café
22. Elegant Restaurant
23. Armada Restaurant

Internet Clubs
1. Troya Internet Club
2. Aladdin Internet Club
3. Discovery Internet Club
4. E Internet Club
5. Internet Club

Museums, Monuments
1. Eternal Flame (WW2 Monument)
2. The Savitsky Karakalpakstan Art Museum
3. Ajiniyaz Monument
4. Friendship of Nations Monument
5. Berdakh Monument
6. Mirza Ulugbek Monument
7. Academy of Arts Exhibition Hall
8. Berdakh Museum

Theatres
1. Amphitheatre
2. Youth Theatre
3. Berdakh Theatre

Banks
1. Kapital Bank
2. National Bank (NBU)
3. Asia Bank
4. Hamkor Bank

- *Tourist Information Centre*
- *Markets (Bazaars)*
- *Hospitals*
- *Fuel (Gas and Oil Stations)*
- *Airport*
R - *Railway Station*
- *Mosque*
- *Entertainment Parks*
- *Lakes*
····· - *Railroad*

A WALK THROUGH NUKUS
ПРОГУЛКА ПО НУКУСУ

Depending on how you arrived in Nukus, this may affect your perception of the city. After getting off a plane you might feel as if you have arrived in the middle of the desert; and after getting off a train or bus, on the contrary, you might have the sensation of arriving in a city.

Nukus is a very young city and a little more than 70 years old. Founded by the Soviets, it looks like many others planned on the drawing board. Along the three main streets Dosnazarov, Turtkul highway and Drujba Narodov Avenue stretches the city centre. The airport is six kilometres north of the centre on Dosnazarov Street, and the train station on this street's southern end.

All along the city runs the Kizketken Water Canal, which in translation means drowned girl, rather ominously. Nukus is also a city of soft contrasts. Besides the new impressive Parliament buildings you will recognize dilapidated prefabricated high-rises as well

В зависимости, на чем вы приехали в Нукус, вас могут одолевать различные чувства от ощущения города. После самолета вы почувствуете, что попали в сердце пустыни, а после поезда или автобуса – наоборот, что вы попали в город после пустыни.

Нукус – город молодой, ему чуть более 70 лет. Внешне Нукус не отличается от многих советских городов. Центр города это три главные улицы, Досназарова, Турткульское шоссе, Дослык гузары, от которых дальше идут небольшие улицы. Аэропорт расположен в 6 км к северу от центра города на ул. Досназарова и железнодорожный вокзал находится в южном конце этой улицы. В городе протекает канал Кызкеткен, что в переводе означает «утонувшая девушка».

Нукус – также город мягких контрастов. Новое здание Парламента, здание Совета Министров украшают центр города, а наряду с панельными многоэтажками вы можете встретить и простые жилища, сделанные из глины.

as simple but charming dwellings made of clay.

Nukus is the administrative capital of Karakalpakstan and also the educational and cultural centre of the region. Young people and students from all over Karakalpakstan come to study at the University, Institutes and different vocational colleges. During national festivities events are held in Nukus in different cultural centres such as the amphitheatre, Berdakh theatre and elsewhere.

The highlight of Nukus and a must-see is the Karakalpakstan State Museum of Art, and widely known as the Savitsky Collection after extraordinary art collector and benefactor Igor Savitsky. The museum hosts the second largest collection of Russian avant garde art in the world after the Russian Museum in St. Petersburg, and the largest collection of Karakalpak folk and applied art and contemporary art originating from Central Asia. The Karakalpak folk art collection contains approximately 9,000 items, including pile rugs, flat weaves, embroidery, jewelry and hand-made textiles and many more. A traditional yurt is also part of the museum's collection, allowing visitors a

Нукус является административной столицей Каракалпакстана, а также образовательным и культурным центром региона. Молодые люди и студенты приезжают со всего Каракалпакстана учиться в Государственном университете им. Бердаха, Педагогическом институте, филиалах Ташкентских университетов и огромных количествах профтехобразовательных колледжей. Национальные праздники проходят в Нукусе в различных культурных местах как амфитеатр, театр им. Бердаха и др.

Главной достопримечательностью Нукуса, конечно, является Музей искусств Республики Каракалпакстан им И.В. Савицкого, более известный, как музей Савицкого в честь экстраординарного коллекционера Игоря Савицкого. В музее располагается вторая по величине коллекция русского авангарда (после Русского музея в Санкт-Петербурге), а также одна из крупнейших коллекций прикладного и древнего искусств народов Центральной Азии.

В коллекцию каракалпакского народно-прикладного искусства входит около 9 тысяч экспонатов, включая ворсовые ковры, узорное ткачество, вышивку, ювелирные украшения, ткани ручной выделки и многое другое. Юрта, украшен-

glimpse of traditional Karakalpak culture.

Besides the impressive Savitsky Collection the Karakalpak State Museum of local Historical Studies provides a good insight into the history, culture, nature and habits of the Karakalpaks. The museum is located inside the Pushkin school and presents its changing exhibitions in two to three rooms while waiting for the construction of a new building.

With the purpose to support local artists the Academy of Arts of Uzbekistan runs an exhibition hall on Turtkul highway which shows in changing exhibitions the work of contemporary Karakalpak artists.

The Berdakh Museum, which is located inside a beautiful building of grey and white Karakalpak marble, opened in honor of the famous Karakalpak poet, holds a collection of his handwritten books and letters as well as books of other famous authors.

Not far from Savitsky's great collection is Amet and Ayimkhan Shamuratova's Home Museum and Guest house, which focuses on a leading couple of Soviet era arts.

ная в традиционном стиле, открывает для туриста необыкновенный мир быта кочевника.

Каракалпакский государственный краеведческий Музей познакомит с историей, культурой, характером и образом жизни каракалпаков. В настоящее время музей находится в школе им. Пушкина и организует временные выставки пока будет построено новое здание музея.

С целью поддержки местных художников Академия художеств Узбекистана проводит выставки работ современных художников Каракалпакстана в выставочном зале который расположен на Турткульском шоссе.

В Музее им. Бердаха, признанного знаменитого поэта Каракалпакстана, в честь которого были названы многие места в Каракалпакстане, можно увидеть коллекцию его рукописных книг и писем, а также книги других известных национальных авторов. Здание музея украшены в серый и белый мрамор, произведенный в Каракалпакстане.

Недалеко от музея им.Савицкого расположен Дом-музей Амета и Аймхан Шамуратовых, и гостиничный дом, который принадлежал паре искусства советской эпохи.

Opening hours:

Karakalpak State Museum of Art/ Savitsky Collection (D8)

Open: Mo-Fr: 9am-5pm, closed 1-2pm, Sa-Su: 10am-4pm
Admission fee: foreign visitors: 15 000 Soum, Guide: 10 000 Soum per person extra

Contact:
① +998-61-222-25-56,
@ museum_savitsky@mail.ru,
www.museum.kr.uz,
www.savitskycollection.org

Karakalpak State Museum of local Historical Studies (D8)

Open: Mo-Fr: 9am-5pm, closed 1-2pm, Sa: 10am-4pm
Admission fee: foreign visitors: 8 000 Soum, Guide: 4 000 Soum per person extra

Contact:
① +998-61-222-73-92,
@ qrdum@mcs.uz,
www.nukus-museum.uz

Academy of Arts of Uzbekistan Exhibition hall (D10/11)

Open: Mo-Fr: 9am-6pm, closed 1-3pm, Sa: 9am-1pm
Free entrance/ no admission fee

Contact:
① +998-61-222-53-10,
@ kk.artacademy@gmail.com

Shamuratova's Home Museum (D7)

Open: Mo-Sa: 9am – 6pm
Admission fee: 2 000 Soum

Contact:
① +998-61-222-34-52,
@ jipek_hotel@rambler.ru

Where to stay in Nukus:

Hotel ARZ (D5)
Close to Airport, clean new furnished rooms, big court-yard with yurts for rent
Price/room: Sg: 40 USD,
Db: 40-60 USD
Contact:
☎ +998-61-222 20 66,
@ hotel.arz@mail.ru

Motel Derbent
City entrance near south station, simple furnished rooms without charm
Prices/room: Sg: 30 USD, Db: 50 USD
Contact:
☎ +998-61-223 26 48,
@ avtokemping@mail.ru

Hotel Jipek Joli 1 (D7) & Jipek Joli 2 (D8)

City center close to Savitksy Museum, JJ1 with traditionally decorated rooms and cosy courtyard, JJ2 is the new and fancy building with comfortable rooms
Prices/room JJ1 & JJ2: Sg: 80 000 - 100 000 Soum, Db: 140 000 – 180 000 Soum
Contact:
☎ +998-61-222 11 00,
@ jipek_hotel@rambler.ru,
www.ayimtour.com

Hotel Kizil Kum (E15)

10 min. to city center, simple modern rooms
Prices/room: Sg: 45-65 USD, Db: 70-100 USD
Contact:
☎ +998-61-223 00 64,
@ info@kizilkumhotel.com,
www.kizilkumhotel.com

Hotel Nukus (D/E9)
City center opposite main post office, simple furnished rooms without charm
Prices/room: Sg: 30-40 USD, Db: 30-40 USD, bed in the dorm: 13 USD
Contact:
☎ +998-61-222 89 41,
@ otel_nukus@mail.ru

Hotel Rahnamo (E9)

City center, modern building with comfortable and pleasant rooms
Prices/room: Sg: 55 USD, Db: 75 USD
Contact:
☎ +998-61-222 47 43,
@ hotelrahnamo@mail.ru

A CONTRIBUTION TO KARAKALPAKSTAN – IGOR V. SAVITSKY

ВКЛАД ИГОРЯ САВИЦКОГО В РАЗВИТИЕ КУЛЬТУРЫ

Igor Savitsky (1915-1984) is truly one of the most outstanding personalities in the modern history of Central Asia. His passion for art and local culture led to the extraordinary rich collection of Russian avant garde art and Karakalpak folk and applied art which can be visited in the Karakalpak State Museum of Art.

Savitsky, who came to Karakalpakstan to participate in the Khorezm Archeological and Ethnographic Expedition in 1950, soon discovered his passion for Karakalpak folk art. Fascinated not only by the Karakalpak art but also by the unique natural landscapes, fishing villages, and patriarchal life he decided to stay in Karakalpakstan and started to collect folk art items wherever he went. During a time when

Игорь Витальевич Савицкий (1915-1984) является действительно одним из самых выдающихся личностей в современной истории Центральной Азии. Его страсть к искусству и местной культуре привели к созданию необычайно богатой коллекции русского авангарда и каракалпакского народно-прикладного искусства. Эту коллекцию можно посмотреть в Каракалпакском государственном музее искусств.

Савицкий, который приехал в Каракалпакстан в составе археолого-этнографической экспедиции Хорезма в 1950 году, вскоре обнаружил свою страсть к каракалпакскому народному искусству. Очарованный не только искусством Каракалпакстана, но и уникальностью природных ландшафтов, рыбацких деревень, и патриархальной жизнью, он решил остаться и где бы он ни был, начал собирать предметы на-

only few understood that he was doing something very valuable for the Karakalpaks the museum was founded in 1966 to exhibit Savitsky's impressive collection of Karakalpak arts.

However, Savitsky had also begun to teach arts to Karakalpak students. For that reason, he started to collect contemporary arts in Tashkent, later on in other cities like Moscow. Without having the initial intention, Savitsky so started to collect forbidden Russian avant garde art and preserved a huge part of the Russian culture, far away from the Soviet authorities in Moscow.

He did not only collect paintings, but also many studies and

родного искусства. Только лишь немногие понимали, что это бесценный вклад в историю Каракллпакстана, и в 1966 году был создан музей для выставки впечатляющей коллекции каракалпакского искусства.

Савицкий также начал преподавать искусство каракалпакским студентам. Именно по этой причине он начал собирать произведения современного искусства в Ташкенте, позже и в других городах, как Москва. Не имея первоначального намерения, Савицкий также начал собирать произведения запрещенного русского авангарда, сохранив огромную часть русской культуры, вдали от советской власти в Москве.

Он не только коллекционировал картины, но и многие исследования

drawings. He was a restless collector, his passion for art and the museum was unlimited. He was doing everything at the museum, from restorations to inventory. He did not care about himself and his health, even slept in the museum and gave up his artistic career as soon as the museum had opened. His life was dedicated to the museum. The formalin he used to clean old bronze items finally damaged his health in such a way, that he had to go to Moscow for medical treatment.

During his treatment in Moscow he managed to collect two tons of art, which were brought to Nukus after Savitsky had died on July 29, 1984.

и рисунки. Он был неугомонным коллекционером, а его страсть к искусству и музею были неограниченными. В музее он делал все, начиная от реставрации заканчивая инвентаризацией. Он не заботился о себе и своем здоровье, даже спал в музее и с открытием музея отказался от своей творческой деятельности. Его жизнь была посвящена музею. Формалин, который он использовал для очистки старых бронзовых изделий, окончательно нанес вред его здоровью, и Савицкий вынужден был уехать в Москву на лечение.

Даже во время его лечения в Москве ему удалось собрать две тонны произведений искусства, которые были привезены в Нукус после смерти Савицкого 29 июля 1984 года.

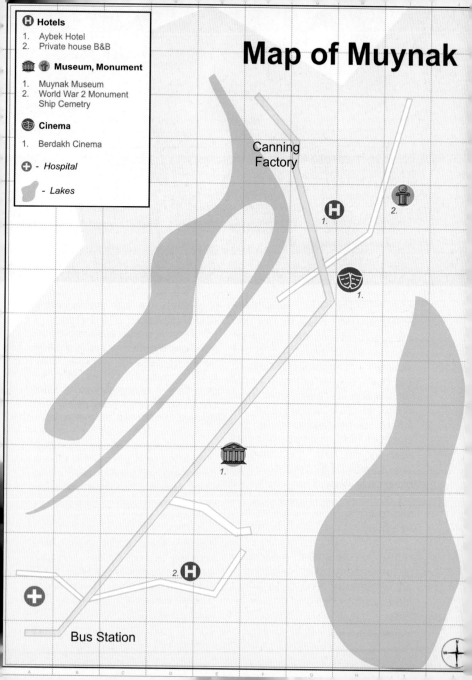

Map of Muynak

H Hotels
1. Aybek Hotel
2. Private house B&B

Museum, Monument
1. Muynak Museum
2. World War 2 Monument
   Ship Cemetry

Cinema
1. Berdakh Cinema

⊕ - *Hospital*

- *Lakes*

Canning
Factory

Bus Station

ECO DISASTER AND TOURISM: ARAL SEA

ЭКОЛОГИЧЕСКОЕ БЕДСТВИЕ И ТУРИЗМ: АРАЛЬСКОЕ МОРЕ

Text based on GIZ-Brochure "The Aral Sea disaster – From living in crisis to solving problems"

на основе брошюры «Катастрофа Аральского моря - жизнь в условиях кризиса и решение проблем» GIZ (Германского Общества по Международному Сотрудничеству).

A trip to the shrinking Aral Sea is an unique experience. Along with the desert environment with white sand dunes and typical desert vegetation, the route leads through the wide Aralkum desert over the Ustyurt Plateau with its scenic landscape formations to the western shores of what is left of the Aral Sea – see recent satellite photos before your visit to see the extent of the damage. This is not a sea known for clear water, pristine beaches or burgeoning fish species, but as a man-made disaster, caused by unsustainable use of resources.

The Aral Sea was once one of the four largest inland lakes in the world. Its northern part is located in Kazakhstan, and its southern part in Karakalpakstan inside Uzbekistan. Since the 1960s the Aral Sea has been steadily

Поездка на высыхающее Аральское море, безусловно, это – приключение, исключительное в своем роде. Наряду с пустынным ландшафтом с белыми барханами и типичной пустынной растительностью, существует маршрут, который ведет через пустыню Аралкум по плато Устюрт с его живописными образованиями ландшафта, к западным берегам того, что осталось от Аральского моря. Перед визитом обязательно посмотрите новейшие фотографии из космоса, чтобы увидеть объем бедствия. Сегодня это море не славится чистой водой, аккуратными пляжами или разнообразием видарыб, а известно как серьезная антропогенная катастрофа, вызванная из-за нерационального использования природных ресурсов.

shrinking and has now declined to 10% of its original size. As a result of constantly expanding irrigation schemes introduced by the Soviets, mainly for the cultivation of rice and cotton, the rivers that fed the Aral Sea could not deliver enough water to balance the annual rate of evaporation and the salinity level. The balance inevitably tipped toward the desiccation of the Aral Sea, leading to a complex catastrophe with serious economical, ecological and social impacts mainly for local populations. The fishing industry broke down when numerous fish species became extinct as the salt content of the receding water increased. High unemployment and emigration followed the loss of 60,000 jobs dependent on the sea. The receding coastline not only gave birth to a new salt-plain desert, the Aralkum, but also had major repercussions on the livelihoods and living conditions of rural populations when a general decline in water quality became common. Severe health problems including respiratory diseases such as asthma and tuberculosis affected the local population.

The regional climate had also changed to colder and longer

Аральское море когда-то было одним из четырех крупнейших внутриматериковых озер в мире. Её северная часть находится на территории Республики Казахстан и её южная часть на территории Каракалпакстана в Республике Узбекистан. С 1960-х годов Аральское море постепенно стало уменьшаться, и её размеры уменьшились до 10% от первоначального размера. В результате постоянного расширения оросительных систем, внедренных правительством Советского Союза, в основном, для выращивания риса и хлопка, реки, которые впадали в Аральское море, больше не доставляли достаточного количества воды в озеро, для того, чтобы сбалансировать годовой показатель испарения и уровень засоленности. Дисбаланс неизбежно вел к высыханию Аральского моря, что привело к сложной катастрофе с серьезными экономическими, экологическими и социальными последствиями, в основном, для местного населения. Рыбная промышленность прекратила свою деятельность, когда многие виды рыб вымерли из-за увеличения содержания солей в исчезающем море. Высокий уровень безработицы и эмиграция повлекли за собой потерю 60.000 рабочих мест завися-

ших от моря. Спад уровня воды не только породил новые территории пустыни Аралкум, но также повлек за собой серьезные последствия для жизни и условий существования сельского населения, когда ухудшение качества воды стало постоянным явлением. Серьезные проблемы со здоровьем, включая заболевания дыхательных путей, таких как астма и туберкулез, распространились среди местного населения.

Региональный климат также изменился: от холодной и долгой зимы до сухого короткого лета, и сейчас ветер поднимает ужасную пыль и соль, неся ущерб местному сельскому хозяйству и уменьшая число видов животного мира в дельтах рек Сырдарьи и Амударьи. Международные усилия сейчас сконцентрировались на стабилизации окружающей среды, в место того чтобы пытаться дать обратный ход уменьшению моря. В пилотном районе в пустынях Аралкум сажаются растения, такие как черный саксаул и травы, которые могут выжить в местности с низким уровнем дождей и высокой соленостью. Хотя этот участок только составляет 1% всей местности, сократились эрозийные ветры и уровень пыли.

winters, and dryer and shorter summers, and winds now carried vicious dust and salt, attacking local agriculture, and greatly reducing the number of species of wildlife in the deltas of the Syr Darya and Amu Darya rivers. International efforts now focus on stabilizing surrounding environments, instead of attempting to reverse the shrinkage of the sea. A pilot area of the Aralkum desert lands are being planted with plants such as Black Saxaul and grasses capable of surviving in areas of low rainfall and high salinity. Though this is just 1% of the total area, erosive winds are scarcer and dust levels slightly reduced.

MUYNAK
МУЙНАК

Formerly a flourishing fishing port, today's city of Muynak is only a shadow of its former self. The inhabitants lived mainly from the fishing industry, but today Muynak is located more than 150 km from the water. After the fish died from saline water and the fish cannery had to close, people deserted Muynak and the region as a whole, with only about 10,000 remaining in the city.

When in the past visitors came to the city with its typical white-blue house facades to rest and relax on the shores of the sea, today they come to see the rusting hulks of fishing vessels laid in the sand. There is also a small museum with exhibits of the cannery as well as impressive pictures of the former fishing works, which can be visited.

A visit to the Aral Sea shore and Muynak city is a two-day trip from Nukus, which should be done with an experienced guide and a 4WD vehicle. There is no

Когда-то процветающий рыбный порт, сегодняшний город Муйнак, является лишь тенью своего прошлого. Люди жили, в основном, за счет рыбной промышленности, но сегодня вода ушла на 150 км от Муйнака. После того, как рыбы вымерли от соленой воды, и рыбоконсервный завод пришлось закрыть, многие люди покинули город Муйнак и ближайшие территории. В настоящее время в самом городе всё ещё проживают 10 000 человек.

Если раньше люди приезжали в Муйнак с обычными бело-голубыми фасадами домов, чтобы отдохнуть и расслабиться на берегу моря, то сейчас они приезжают, чтобы увидеть остатки загнивающих рыболовных судов, стоящих на песке. Здесь есть музей с экспонатами существовавшего ранее консервного завода, где можно увидеть впечатляющие фотографии прежнего рыболовства.

accommodation and most tour guides rent out tents for camping. As the wind can be very cold at night in this area, it is advisable to do the Aral Sea trip between April and October.

Overnight in Muynak:

Hotel Oybek
Very simple accommodation facilities with shared bathroom from Soviet times located in the city centre close to the Ship cemetery

Homestays can be arranged by Sagijan Aytjanov,
☽ +998-93-920-01-55,
@ saitjanov@yahoo.com
Octyabr Dospanov,
☽ +998-90-575-32-28,
@ oktyabrd@gmail.com

Muynak exhibition
Open: Mo-Fr: 10am-6pm, closed 1-2pm, Sa-Su:
Admission fee: foreign visitors: 8 000 Soum
☽ +998-…??????????????????????

Поездку из Нукуса на Аральское море можно осуществить за два дня с опытным гидом на внедорожнике. На Аральском море нет условия для жилья, и поэтому большинство организаторов поездки сдают в аренду палатки для кемпинга. Самое удобное время посещения Аральского моря период с апреля по октябрь, в остальное время погодные условия затруднят насладиться впечатлениями.

HIDDEN LIVES BETWEEN DESERTS: FLORA & FAUNA OF KARAKALPAKSTAN

СКРЫТАЯ ЖИЗНЬ МЕЖДУ ПУСТЫНЬ: ФЛОРА И ФАУНА КАРАКАЛПАКСТАНА

Most of Karakalpakstan is desert: the Ustyurt and the Kyzylkum, and between them the Aral Sea and Amu Darya river delta have in turn developed another new desert, the Aralkum. The Kyzylkum, or red sands, desert stretches between the rivers Amu Darya in the south and Syr Darya in the north, and the Karakalpak part covers about six million hectares. The surface of the north west Kyzylkum varies, with most of it hilly sands, dunes of different sizes. The desert merges in its north western part with the new Aralkum desert. Many of the wet salt marshes of Aralkum are situated on former bays within the sea, and the surface is made up in part with salt crust up to five centimetres thick.

The Ustyurt plateau is an elevated plain up to almost 300 metres high

Большая часть территории Каракалпакстана является пустыней: плато Устюрт и Кызылкум. Между территорией Аральского моря и дельтой реки Амударьи возникла новая пустыня - Аралкум.

Полупустыня Кызылкум (красный песок) протянулась между реками Амударья на юге и Сырдарья на севере. Кызылкум занимает около 6,0 млн. Га на территории Республики Каракалпакстан. Поверхность этого Северо-Западного Кызылкума разнообразна, большую часть территории занимают бугристые пески, барханы, а между ними разного размера такыры и саи. Пустыня Кызылкумы в северо-западной части слилась с новой пустыней Аралкум. Однако значительная часть Аралкумов

with a number of drainage basins. This remote area has maintained an almost pristine wildlife environment including rare species as it is largely uninhabited and cannot be reached either by paved roads or by railway. About 600 known species of vascular plants can be found, among others desert ephemerals or the well adapted saxaul tree (haloxylon ammodendron). Among mammals some rare and red listed species are living on the Ustyurt, such as the long-spined hedgehog, Turkmenistan caracal, corsac fox, steppe polecat, gazelle, antelope and Ustyurt sheep. And during different seasons more than 200 km species of birds can be seen on the Ustyurt, with about a quarter nesting there. These are mainly passerine birds and birds of prey.

An extraordinary bird life can be watched in the Sudochie wetland in spring (mid March to mid May) and autumn (September, October). This large lake system is the primary nesting habitat for many species of birds and migratory birds stopping on the West Asian migration route. In 2007 Sudochie was included in a global list of important bird areas. The Sudochie wetland is located to the north of Kungrad, about 220 from Nukus city, and consists of a large number of small and four large reservoirs and adjoining areas.

представлена мокрыми солончаками на месте бывших заливов, а также песчано-глинисты-ми солончаками. Поверхность бывает покрыта мощными солевыми корками до 5 см толщиной.

Плато Устюрт представляет собой сплошную возвышенную равнину высотой до 300 м и рядом дренажных бассейнов. Плато является отдаленным необитаемым районом, к которой сложно добраться, что дает ей сохранить совершенно нетронутой фауну редких видов. Во флоре известны около 600 видов высших сосудистых растений, среди которых наряду с эфемерными растениями очень хорошо приспособился саксаул (haloxylon ammodendron) Среди млекопитающих можно встретить редкие виды, внесенные в список Красной книги Узбекистана и в списки Красной книги Международного союза охраны природы, к которым относятся длинноиглый еж, туркменский каракал, корсак, степной хорь, джейран, сайгак и устюртский баран. На Устюрте, в различные сезоны года, можно встретить более 200 видов птиц, из которых гнездятся не более 52 видов. Это в основном воробьи и хищные птицы.

The valley and delta of the Amu Darya is characterized by a peculiar tugai landscape. This globally unique desert flood-plain forest emerges in arid steppes and lowland in Central Asia and contains river bed gallery forests, reeds, drought-resistant bushes and grass. Among the deserts and semi-deserts of Central Asia tugais provide the natural habitat for a rich diversity of species. Due to a sharp reduction in regulation of river flow, the development of irrigated farming areas, the formerly 300,000 hectares of riparian woodlands have been reduced to a mere 33,000 hectares in Karakalpakstan and the formerly widespread tugai landscape was pushed back.

In response, the Lower Amu-Darya Biosphere Reserve had been created with the purpose of conservation of the typical intrazonal tugai ecosystem. Within the Biosphere Reserve the Badai Tugai Nature Reserve exists to guard the world's largest population of the rare Bukhara deer. The reserve is a protection zone and is therefore not accessible for visitors. Nevertheless, there are buffer zones which are accessible and in this way tugai forests and related biodiversity.

Весной (с середины марта до середины мая) и осенью (в сентябре, октябре) на Озере Судочье можно наблюдать экстраординарную жизнь птиц. Озеро Судочье является основным местом обитания многих видов птиц и остановки перелётных птиц на западно-Азиатском миграционном пути во время миграций, среди которых имеются редкие и исчезающие виды птиц. Озеро Судочье расположено в северной части Кунградского района, в 220 км от города Нукуса, состоит из большого количества маленьких озер и четырех больших резервуаров и прилегающих зон.

Долина и дельта реки Амударьи характеризуется своеобразным тугайным ландшафтом. Это глобально уникальные пойменные леса возникают в засушливых степях и низменностях Центральной Азии и содержат в руслах реки галерейные леса, тростники, засухоустойчивые кустарники и травы. Среди пустыни и полупустыни Центральной Азии тугайные леса обеспечивают естественную среду обитания для богатого разнообразия видов. В Каракалпакстане в связи с резким сокращением в регулировании речного стока, развитием орошаемого земледелия, площади тугайных лесов сократилась от 300 тыс. га до 33 тыс. га.

Как ответ был создан Нижне-Амударьинский Биосферный Резерват с целью сохранения и устойчивого использования ресурсов, был создан государственный заповедник Бадай-Тугай. Значение заповедника Бадай-тугай велико как хранителя самой большой в мире популяции бухарского оленя , резерва-

ций защитной зоны и следовательно, не доступна для посетителей. Тем не менее, существуют буферные зоны, которые являются доступными для посещения. К примеру, для знакомства с тугайными лесами и биологическим разнообразием природы, можно посетить территории буферных зон в Берунийском и Амударьинском районах (южный Каракалпакстан) и на северной части в Кегелийском, Караузякском районах.

RELIGION & SACRED PLACES
РЕЛИГИЯ & САКРАЛЬНЫЕ МЕСТА

Since the 8th century when the Sassanid Empire was conquered by the Arabs, the main religion in Karakalpakstan as in other Central Asian countries is Islam. Although sites of pilgrimage in Karakalpakstan do not always relate to Muslim belief, people still revere these places of folk memory.

Such places of worship are the sacred tree in Shamuratova Street in Nukus and the Jantemir Ishan monument situated about 30 km from Kungrad on the way to Muynak where drivers stop to pray for a safe trip. The dried mulberry tree and the woman sitting next to it are frequented throughout the year by people for any number of reasons, to have a baby, for luck when entering university or for when they dream of dead relatives.

A major pilgrimage destination for local people is the impressive complex of Sultan Uvays Bobo. The site is worth a visit for its good view of this region and to get an understanding of local beliefs by observing the pilgrims and their

Начиная с 8 века, когда империя Сасанидов была завожена арабами, основной религией в Каракалпакстане, как и в других странах Центральной Азии, стал ислам. Нельзя сказать, что все святые места, к которым поклоняются каракалпаки, связаны с религией ислам.

Таким местом поклонения являются **«святое дерево»** по улице Шамуратова и памятник Жантемир Ишану, расположенное в 30 км от Кунграда, по трассе Кунград-Муйнак. Святое дерево, высохший тутовник и женщина, которая читает коран, принимает посетителей круглый год по различным поводам, как например рождение ребенка, поступление в ВУЗ, или даже когда усопшие родственники снятся во сне.

Одним из главных мест паломничества для местных жителей является внушительный комплекс Султан Увайс Бобо. Эта достопримечательность достойна внимания, можно сделать обзор региона, чтобы иметь представление о местной

ritual offerings. Located close to the city of Biruniy the site is covered by a large cemetery surrounding the mausoleum of Sultan Uvays-al-Qarani, locally known as Sultan Uvays Bobo. The mausoleum dates back to the 9th century CE, but the present structure mainly had been constructed between 17th and 19th century.

After leaving the rest area where pilgrims buy drinks and sit down to share food, you reach the mausoleum, but further on in the mountains is the most holy place which is supposed to contain the foot and knee prints of the Sultan.

Another site considered as a holy place is the old Sufi centre Iyshan-Kala, dating from the 19th century. As a religious and educational centre it was meant to instruct young boys in the teaching of the Koran. Besides the study of the Islamic religion the young students were also taught sciences. The centre consisted of living houses as well as religious and educational institutions and others and was run by an iyshan, a Sufi religious leader. The ruins of the houses, study rooms as well as the mosque can still be visited. The madrasah and its respectively leader (Iyshan) played several times an important role as protector against Turkmen invaders as well as political centre against the Soviet power. Later

религии, понаблюдать за паломниками и их ритуалами. Комплекс расположен недалеко от города Бируни, в основном состоит из большого кладбища, окружающий мавзолей Султана Увайс-аль-Карани, локально известный как Султан Увайс Бобо. Мавзолей датируется IX веком нашей эры, но нынешняя структура в основном была построена между XVII-XIX вв.

Паломники на территории мавзолея могут купить напитки и поделиться едой, после этой зоны , вы достигнете мавзолей, а еще далее в горах вы можете увидеть самое почитаемое святое место, следы самого Султана, отпечатанные на камне

Еще одним святым местом является старый центр суфизма, памятник XIX века Ишан-кала. Он являлся религиозным образовательным центром, в котором молодые люди изучали Коран. Наряду с изучением религии ислам, ученики обучались и другим наукам. Центр состоял из жилых домов, а также религиозных и образовательных учреждений и других, и находился в управлении ишана, суфийского религиозного лидера. И сегодня можно посетить руины домов, учебных кабинетов, мечеть. Медресе и его уважаемый лидер играли важную роль в защите от туркменских захватчиков, а также послужили политическим центром против Советской власти. Позже в советское время учебный

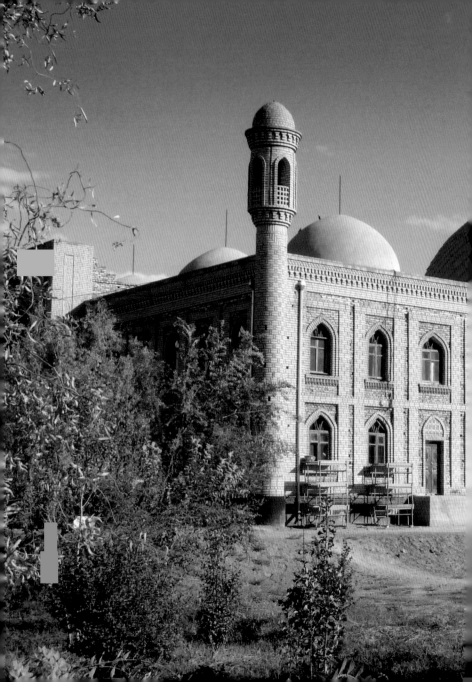

during Soviet times the educational centre was abandoned. Iyshan-Kala is located in the outskirts of the city Xalqabad, which is about 25 km from Nukus on the road to Chimbai. When entering Xalqabat, right after the town sign, turn right onto the street. Continue for 2 km and follow the farm track on the right.

However, Zoroastrianism was the leading religion in pre-Islamic Khorezm. This religious philosophy goes back to the teachings of the prophet Zoroaster and the holy scripture Avesta. In the centre of the faith were the two opposing forces: Ahura Mazda (Illuminating Wisdom) and Angra Mainyu (Destructive Spirit). Zoroastrians believe that the elements are pure and that fire represents God's light or wisdom. They communally worship in a fire temple.

Zoroasters ideas led to a powerful religion which probably developed between 1800 BCE and 600 BCE and widespread over Persia (Iran) and Central Asia. Findings such as fire temples, household articles, ceramic objects and sculptures discovered in the ruins of the desert castle Toprak-Kala and others as well as the monument Chilpik - a tower of silence - relate to Zoroastrianism and Avesta characters. Also the official holiday Nowruz, the New Year's Festival, dates back to Zoroastrianism.

центр Ишан-калы был заброшен. Ишан кала находится в предместий города Халкабад, в 25 км от Нукуса трассы Нукус-Чимбай. После въезда в город Халкабад, после вывески с названием города, вы можете повернуть направо, и после 2 км вы увидете памятник.

Однако, зороастризм был ведущей религией доисламского Хорезма. Эта религиозная философия восходит к учению пророка Зороастра и священного писания Авеста. В центре религии борятся две противоположные силы: Ахурамазда (Освещаюшая мудрость) и Ангра-Майнью, Ахриман (Дух разрушения). Зороастрийцы считают, что природные элементы чисты и что огонь представляет Божьй свет или Мудрость. Они обшиной поклонялись храму огня. Идея Зороастризма привело к мошной религии, которая возможно развилась между 1800-600 г. до н.э и распространилась на территории Персии (Ирана) и Центральной Азии. Такие находки как храмы огня, предметы домашнего обихода, керамические предметы и скульптуры, обнаруженные в развалинах замка Топрак кала и другие, такие как монумент Чилпык- башня молчания, свидетельствуют о существовании в регионе религии зороастризма. Более того, официальный праздник Навруз, праздник наступления Нового года, корнями уходит в Зороастризм

**Tours to the Aral Sea & Muynak, historical sights
and pilgrimage sites can be organized by:**

Ayimtour/ Jipek Joli Hotel
☽ +998-61-222-11-00,
@ jipek_hotel@rambler.ru,
www.ayimtour.com

Ayaz-Kala Tur
☽ +998-61-350 59 09, +998-61-532 43 61,
ayazkala_tur@mail.ru

Sihaya Tours
☽ +998-93-920-90-10,
@ uzguides@gmail.com

Oktyabr Dospanov
☽ +998-90-575-32-28,
@ oktyabrd@gmail.com

FOLK TRADITIONS, CEREMONIES AND CELEBRATIONS
НАРОДНЫЕ ТРАДИЦИИ, ОБРЯДЫ И ПРАЗДНИКИ

The Karakalpak as an ethnic group have their own rituals and traditions, which differ from others in richness and originality. Karakalpak kinship is not only determined by blood but by clan affiliation. There are 14 large clans, which are in turn subdivided into smaller ones. Belonging to a clan branch means membership by blood and prohibition of marriage between clan siblings. Therefore, when young people are meeting, they are especially interested in their clan affiliation, which can also be a source of mirth: people make fun of the idea that, if you are interested in clan history, it may turn out to prove that your husband or wife is your relative.

Bride-napping is a staple feature for Western media, and though the criminal and cruel practice no longer exists, an anodyne nod to this former custom remains. Today there are two forms of marriage arrangement:

Каракалпаки как народность имеют свои обряды и традиции, отличающиеся богатством и своеобразием истории народа. У каракалпаков родственная связь определяется не только кровными узами, но по клановой принадлежности. Существуют 14 больших кланов, которые в свою очередь подразделяются на более мелкие. Принадлежность к одной клановой ветке считается кровным родством, и запрещаются браки между ними. Поэтому молодежь при знакомстве в первую очередь интересуется, к какому клану принадлежит избранник или избранница. По этому поводу существует много шуток и анекдотов. Посмеиваются, что если интересоваться историей клана жены, она тоже, в конце концов, может оказаться твоей родственницей.

Интересно также создание семьи у каракалпаков. Бытует много зна-

a mock-stealing after agreement, and matchmaking. The former largely dispenses with prohibitive dowries, meaning it can often be an option due to economic reasons. The average age of marriage lies between 18 to 21 years for girls and 25 to 28 years for young men.

An important role in keeping the traditions alive is the festive day toy. Regardless of the reason to celebrate - a wedding, an anniversary, a birthday, a bride's arrival or a child's birth - any positive event in the life of the family is marked by a toy. The Besik Toy is the ceremony for the giving of the cradle and is the first important event for a family. When the first child is born to a family the bride's family usually donates the cradle. Not less valuable is the ceremony in honour of the circumcision of the family's son. Usually the circumcision will be done at the age five or seven.

Weddings are in every culture a very particular ceremony. For this special day the Karakalpaks kept the new tradition of an outing from Soviet times, meaning a motorcade of decorated vehicles will follow the young couple during a trip to important places and monuments around the city, where photographs are taken. But before starting this trip the rite of Betashar is performed, the so-called opening of the bride's

менитых легенд о похищении невесты. В той дикой форме похищение невесты уже не существует. Форма осталась прежней - похищение, но содержание полностью изменилось. Это означает, что в настоящее время существует две формы создания семьи: Похищение по договоренности, и сватовство. Выбрать форму - это лишь экономический вопрос, похищение по договоренности дешевле обходятся молодым, чем сватовство. Средний возраст замужества и женитьбы между 18-21 годом для девушек, 25-28 лет для молодых людей.

Большую роль в соблюдении традиций играет праздник «Той», независимо от того, свадьба, юбилей, день рождения, проводы невесты, рождение ребенка, любое положительное событие в жизни семьи обозначают этим словом – «Той».

Важными в жизни семьи считается Бесик Той – праздник колыбели. Когда рождается первый ребенок родственниками со стороны невесты принято дарить колыбель. Также немаловажен праздник в честь обрезания сына. Обычно обрезание происходит в нечетном возрасте в 5 или 7 лет.

Из советского наследия каракалпаки получили новую традицию «Гулянка», которая происхо-

face by a singer or presenter who recites special instructions for the bride, who then bows to each family member and gains through this the guarantee of a happy life.

As in other countries in this part of the world, the main holiday for the Karakalpaks is the Zoroastrian festival of Nowruz, which is normally held on or around 21 March when the first day of spring and the awakening of nature is celebrated. Festivities are held throughout the night, while sumalak, the porridge of Nowruz made from wheat germ, is prepared in large pots.

On 9 May the day of memorial is usually celebrated. Families head to the cemetery to pay tribute to deceased relatives and to clean their graves. Muslims are not supposed to go often to graves, but they are allowed to go there on certain dates, as it is believed that the graves of the ancestors should not be left to ruin. The tradition of burial is also different from many other nations. During three days the deceased persons are mourned, and usually on the third day, depending on the weather, they will be buried. During this period people are coming and going to the house in question, in accordance with mourning rules. While the dead person is laid out in his house, all women of his family are sitting in a room and lament loudly.

дит в день свадьбы. Кортеж машин украшенных лентами, шарами и куклами можно встретить на улицах города. До гулянки производится обряд «Беташар», что в переводе обозначает «Открытие лица невесты», баксы готовит текст наставление для невесты, какой она должна быть, чтобы жить счастливо.

Основным праздником каракалпаков считается праздник идущий корнями в зороастризм, праздник «Навруз», празднование первого дня весны и пробуждения природы. «Навруз» празднуют 21 марта, все выходят на площадь, происходит народное гулянье, всю ночь всей улицей готовят «сумалак» из проросшей пшеницы, готовят также «Наурыз гоже» - кашу Навруза.

Широко распространен день памяти, празднуемые ежегодно 9 мая. Все люди в этот день устремляются к кладбищу, где похоронены близкие люди, дают дань памяти усопшим родственникам и ухаживают за их могилами. Примечательно, что у мусульман нельзя часто ходить на могилу, разрешается ходить только по определенным датам, считается, что нельзя топтать могилы наших предков. Традиция похорон также отличается от многих других народов. Три дня оплакивается мертвый, в зависимости от погоды на третий день

The louder they lament, the more obvious they feel the grief. Men enter the house uttering short cries, and women must weep and embrace each relative of the deceased.

Family celebrations and funerals can see around 1,000 people participating, including all friends and neighbors, with dozens served meals at the same time throughout the day.

обычно хоронится. Принято, что мужчины заходят в дом умершего, издавая плач, а женщины тоже должны плакать, обнявшись с каждой родственницей погибшего. Очень важно, чтобы в семье среди детей были мальчики и девочки. Девочки сидят в ряд, оплакивая усопшего, а сыновья должны с плачем запускать новых людей. Обычно на торжествах и похоронах участвуют до тысячи человек.

KARAKALPAK HANDICRAFTS & EPIC HERITAGE
ВОЗРОЖДЕНИЕ КАРАКАЛПАКСКИХ РЕМЕСЕЛ

The Karakalpaks have a long and rich history influenced by a semi-nomadic lifestyle. Some Karakalpaks settled in the Aral Sea region, while others remained nomads. These different lifestyles are reflected in handicraft patterns, including tent bands, yurts, wood carving, embroidery, jewellery, leather stamping and musical instruments, often reflecting their environment. In nomadic patterns you can find motifs of waves and imitations of living creatures such

Полукочевой образ жизни повлиял на богатую и длительную историю каракалпаков. Отличительный образ жизни наложил своеобразный отпечаток на развитие каракалпакского ремесла, что делает его еше более уникальным. Образцы традиционных каракалпакских ремесел, в том числе палатки с каймой, юрты, резьба по дереву, вышивка, ювелирные изделия, кожаные изде-

as crows and fishes, as well as frogs, a traditional pre-Islamic totem, related to water and also a symbol for fertility.

Some of this cultural heritage was lost over the years, but during the 1990s the Karakalpak government paid attention to the revival of traditional culture and handicrafts. Craftsmen were encouraged and supported to produce traditional crafts; historians, ethnographers and designers held seminars to improve the understanding of Karakalpak culture among craftsmen. Trainings about the production of traditional handicrafts also took place at the Savitsky Museum. Eventually, craftsmen started not only to copy the techniques and styles of old handicrafts, but to develop new products like souvenirs, and in that way adapt the old traditions to modern life. The five handicrafts that were chosen to be revived within the program were embroidery; weaving; yurts; wood carving; and musical instruments. Thanks to this initiative, most of these handicrafts have been successfully revived and are currently flourishing.

And even if the meanings of the wonderful patterns on carpets, wood or embroidered items might remain unknown for most

лия с тиснеными узорами и музыкальные инструменты часто отражали окружающую среду. В образах кочевников вы можете найти мотивы волн и имитации живвых сушеств, таких как, ворона и рыба. Также, встречаются изображения лягушки, считавшиеся традиционными доисламскими тотемами, которые связаны с водой и являются символом плодородия.

Некоторые из этого богатого культурного наследия были утрачены за последние годы. В 1990-е годы каракалпакское правительство решило обратить внимание на возрождение традиционной культуры и ремесел. Ремесленников поощряли и поддерживали в процессе производства традиционных ремесел. Историки, этнографы и дизайнеры проводили семинары среди искусных мастеров (ремесленников) для повышения понимания каракалпакской культуры. В музее Савицкого проводились тренинги, обучающие производству традиционных ремесел. Со временем, мастера начали не только копировать стиль и способы производства древнего ремесла, но

outsiders, the mysticism and beauty of traditional ornaments and combination of colors will always succeed in captivating the visitors.

Traditional Karakalpak music relates back to the old tradition of bards transmitting the epic heritage of the mythical world of nomads when they were still systematically invited to weddings. During that time the bard played a very important role in the traditional Karakalpak society as the bearer of knowledge that has been passed on from one generation to another.

Two different types of singers – the jiraw and the baqsi - had been responsible to narrate epics and stories about love and the quest for love as well as heroes and their achievements in major combats. Those epics, among them the famous Alpamis epic and the Kyrgys epic (40 girls), are narratives that last several hours, and at times several nights.

The very special style of throat singing is used by the jiraw, together with the two-string fiddle, the qobiz, supporting his recitation of heroic epics. As for the baqsi, his music stems from a rather different style. He sings epic poems about courtly love in a natural voice, and accompanies himself with a two-string lute, the duwtar.

и стали разрабатывать современные изделия, например, сувениры. Таким образом, адаптировав древние традиции, они показывали жизнь древних каракалпаков. В рамках программы для возрождения были выбраны пять ремесел, которыми являются вышивка, ткачество, юрты, резьба по дереву и музыкальные инструменты. Благодаря этой инициативе, большинство из этих ремесел успешно возрождаются и процветают в настоящее время.

Даже если значение уникальных и прекрасных узоров на коврах, деревянных или вышитых изделиях остаются незнакомыми для большинства неспециалистов, мистика и красота традиционных украшений, сочетание цветов всегда очаровывает посетителей.

Традиционная каракалпакская музыка относится к старой традиции бардов передачи эпического наследия мифического мир кочевников. Их систематически приглашали на свадьбы. Бард играл очень важную роль в традиционном обществе каракалпасков как передат-

Although the interest of young people in studying the work of the bard is undeniable, today's bards are much less often solicited to perform during weddings. They can therefore only be observed during concerts abroad, festivals and competitions, as well as national commemorations, during which their performances rarely exceed ten minutes.

Handicraft with traditional Karakalpak embroidery can be bought in:

Museum Shop inside Savitsky Museum (D0)
Open: Mo-Fr: 9am-5pm, closed 1-2pm, Sa-Su: 10am-4pm
Contact:
① +998-61-222-25-56,
@ museum_savitsky@mail.ru

Workshop Karakalpak Style (D7)
Across from Hotel Jipek Joli 1
Open during season (mid March to mid November): Mo-Sa: 10am-7pm, or upon request
Contact:
① +998-61-222-01-01,
+998-90-658-61-88
(Ziyada Sambetova)

Instruments can be purchased in a small shop inside the big bazaar building (close to the booths where fresh salads are sold).

чик устного народного творчества, от одного поколения к другому.

Два разных певцав – жырау и бахсы, были ответственны за передачу следующему поколению эпосов и историй о любви, также героях и их достижениях в сражениях. Такие эпосы, как Алпамыс и 40 девушек, были повествовательны и для их исполнения, требовалось несколько часов, а порой и несколько ночей. Жырау использует особый стиль горлового пения, вместе с двуструнной скрипкой, кобыз, поддерживая декламацию героических эпосов. Бахсы использует иной стиль. Он поет эпические поэмы о любви обычным голосом, аккомпанируя двуструнный дутар.

Несомненно молодые люди до сих пор заинтересованы в изучении данного жанра, но на сегодняшний день их реже приглашают на свадьбы. Следовательно *жырау* и *бахсы* можно послушать только во время концертов за рубежом, во время фестивалей и конкурсов, национальных празднеств и их выступления редко превышают десять минут.

KARAKALPAK CUISINE - FOOD AND BEVERAGES

КАРАКАЛПАКСКАЯ КУХНЯ - ЕДА И НАПИТКИ

A well known proverb says that in order to survive Karakalpak needs: three months of melon, three months of dairy products, three months of pumpkin and three months of fish. The Karakalpak cuisine is nourishing, however the consumption of meat and animal products is dominant. Consequently the majority of dishes are meat based.

Traditional dishes are prepared in one pot using the slow cooking method. This is due to the fact that the former semi-nomadic lifestyle of the population did not allow for carrying around too much stuff and so, the preparation of dishes was adapted to the lifestyle. Besides plov other typical dishes one should try are: Gurtik also known as Besh Barmak (boiled noodles and vegetables with boiled meat on top, served on a big plate and usually eaten with five fingers), Juuyeri Gurtik (Besh Barmak made out of sorghum), Kuuyrdak (stir fried noodles and

Пословица гласит: каракалпакам для выживания необходимы: три месяца дыни, три месяца – молочной продукции, три месяца – тыквы, три месяца рыбы. Каракалпакская кухня богата питательными веществами. Почти все блюда готовятся с мясом.

Для каракалпакской кухни характерно приготовление пищи в одной посуде. Это объясняется, тем, что издревле каракалпаки вели полукочевой образ жизни. Не всегда приходилось иметь возможность использовать разную посуду для приготовления пищи. Наряду с пловом вы можете попробовать гуртик, более известный как Бешбармак (вареная лапша и овощи с вареным мясом, подается на большой тарелке и обычно едят руками, бешбармак в переводе означает «пять пальцев»), жууери гуртик (бешбармак из сорго), кууырдак (жареная картошка с мясом), майек борек (фар-

vegetables), Mayek-Borek (dough stuffed with eggs), Aksaulak (dry and precooked noodles to put in a broth, usually served at big events to take care big amounts of guests quickly and easily), Kyrmysh (moon shaped fried dumpling filled with ground beef or vegetables), Manty (steamed dumplings filled with minced meat), Kes bass (noodle soup) and Mashaba (a soup made out of rice, kidney beans, green gram).

Fish has traditionally been a staple food of the Karakalpak people, due to the abundant supply which could be found in the Aral Sea as well as the rivers. The main type of fish is carp; also it is very popular and used for preparing the tasty fish soup or fried fish. Trying these famous fish dishes is a highlight of one's stay in Karakalpakstan. The biggest variety of fish dishes can be found in the district of Muynak, from fish burgers to fish plov. It is common for the local population to serve these dishes to guests in their home.

The main meal for the Karakalpaks is reserved for the evening when the whole family sits together around the dastarkhan, the space where food is served. Usually the eldest member of the family starts the meal. If you are lucky to be invited as guest to a wedding or any other family

шированные в тесте яйца), акса-улак (сухая лапша в мясном бульоне, обычно используется на больших мероприятиях, для быстрого обслуживания гостей), кырмыш (жареное тесто в форму полумесяца, заполненные говяжьим фаршем), манты (большие пельмени на пару с начинкой из мяса), кесбас (суп с лапшой) и машаба (суп из риса, фасоли и маша)

Рыба, особенно сазан (карп) очень популярна в регионе, в основном это уха из рыбы и жареная рыба. Разнообразие рыбных блюд можно увидеть в Муйнакском районе Республики. От рыбных котлет до рыбного плова можно попробовать в гостях в Муйнаке.

Основной прием пиши у каракалпаков приходится на вечер, когда вся семья после трудового будня собирается к дастархану. Обязательное условие ужина – дождаться всех. Обычно трапезу начинает старший в семье. Если вас пригласили в гости, на свадьбу или какое-нибудь мероприятие, не удивляйтесь обилию дастархана, где одновременно вы можете увидеть и закуску, и блюдо, и мучные изделия, и соленья, и салаты, и сухофрукты, и десерт. Обязательно принято подавать баурысаки - жареное тесто. Обычно

event, you will be presented with a richly decorated and set dastarkhan. Bauyrsak – fried dough will be served, usually placed strategically so that there is no more free space seen on the table. The custom is to sit on the floor around the long and low placed tables on mattresses, called Kurpatchas.

Green tea is usually served during the meals or, depending on the type of food, black tea with milk. It is a particular style of black tea where fresh milk will be boiled together with the black tea and served with sweets. During the very hot summer slightly salted drinks such as Ashygan (sour creamery drink made by fermentation) and Ayran (not fermented dairy drink, with less fat) are very popular and effective in quenching your thirst.

Vodka is also very popular tipple, especially during weddings and other celebrations. The most popular is the Qarataw-Vodka, which is a local product manufactured in a vodka factory in Nukus. The locals take pride in the fact that the equipment for the vodka factory was brought to Nukus after the WWII, to only two places in the Soviet Union of which Nukus is one. The vodka has a mild taste, the locals say that if you stick only to vodka during the evening, the next day should suffer from a headache.

принято, чтобы на столе не было свободного места. Также принято сидеть на полу, куда стелется «курпача» (ватные одеяла).

Во время приема пищи обычно подается зеленый чай, или в зависимости от вида пищи, черный чай с молоком. Это особый стиль заваривания черного чая, когда свежее молоко варится с черным чаем и подается со сладостями. Во время жаркого сезона популярны такие напитки слабосоленые напитки как Ашыган (кислый-молочный напиток, приготовленный путем брожения) и Айран (кисло-молочный напиток без брожения, с меньшим количеством жира), которые очень хорошо утоляют жажду.

Водка в регионе также популярна, особенно им сервируют стол во время свадеб и других праздничных мероприятий. Водка Каратау является местным продуктом и производится в Нукусе. Говорят, что оборудование винно-водочного завода была поставлена после второй мировой войны только в двух местах Советского Союза, одно из которых Нукус. Водка Каратау имеет мягкий вкус, и если вы весь вечер пили Каратау, завтра вы не почувствуете головной боли.

Where to eat in Nukus

Local cuisine and traditional Karakalpak dishes:
(order in advance)
Cafe Palwan-Shakh (D7), +998-61-222 62 67
(Egg stuffed doughs)
Sheraton (E9), +998-61-222-87-81
Merlion (C10), +998-61-224 28 93
Neo (D9), +998-61-224-00-03
Cafe Kann (G14), +998-61-223-74-80

Caucasian cusine:
Mona Lisa (C9), Tel.: +998-61-224-06-32
Kaukasian Shashlik (B10)
ARS Cafe (F10)

Fish restaurants:
Cafe Okean (H11), +998-61-223-66-73
Sevintsch, 4-5 km north of airport
Azim, 4-5 km north of airport

Korean cuisine, pizza, cakes & coffee:
Sonata Cafe (H13/14)

USEFUL INFORMATION
ПОЛЕЗНАЯ ИНФОРМАЦИЯ

Visa/ import and export regulations

Visa regulations as well as import and export regulations for Uzbekistan are valid. Check with your Ministry of Foreign Affairs for detailed information. There are the common international import and export bans on weapons, ammunition, drugs, precious stones, art works and antiques of historical value. Furthermore, there are restrictions on imports/exports of tobacco, alcohol and foreign currency. On arrival a customs declaration in duplicate should be filled in, which has to be presented at departure again. Information about visa can be found on http://mfa.uz/eng/consular_issues/

Registration

Uzbek rules ask foreigners to register during three days after arrival at the local Office for Visa and Registration (OViR). Upon check-in into a hotel, the hotel will take care of your registration and provide you with a registration slip. If you stay in a private home, you and your host are responsible

Виза / положение об импорте и экспорте

Существует визовое положение, а также положение об импорте и экспорте. Обратитесь в Министерство иностранных дел для подробной информации. Существуют общие международные запреты на импорт и экспорт: оружия, боеприпасов, наркотиков, дорогих камней, работ искусства и антиквариатов исторической ценности. Далее, существуют ограничения на импорты/экспорты табачных изделий, алкоголя и иностранной валюты. При прибытии должны быть заполнены две копии таможенной декларации, одна из которых должна быть представлена во время отбытия. Информация можно найти на http://mfa.uz/rus/

Регистрация

Законы Республики Узбекистан требуют иностранцев зарегистрироваться в Отделе Виз и Регистрации (ОВИР) в течение трех дней после вашего прибытия. Во время регистрации в гостинице, представители гостиницы должны заняться вашей регистрацией в ОВИРе и предоставить вам регистрационную карточку. Если в остановитесь в частном доме, то

for the registration with the next local OViR-office.

Entering Karakalpakstan (Nukus)

By plane: Direct international flights from Moscow (Russia) only. Domestic flights from Tashkent twice a day are operated by Uzbekistan Airways.

By train: Trains from/ to Tashkent operate several times a week; there are direct connections with Moscow, St.-Petersburg, Saratow (Russia), Dushanbe, Khoudjant (Tadjikistan) and Almaty (Kazakhstan).

By bus: From Tashkent via Samarkand and Bukhara twice a day. No border crossing busses.

Airport (E5)

The airport is located in the North of Nukus on Dosnazarov St. about a 10 minute drive from the city centre.

Air tickets "Aviakassa" (D8/9, E7)

Foreigners must pay for their flight tickets in cash in US Dollar and should bring two copies of their passport. Tickets may also be purchased at the airport.

вы и те, кто вас принимает ответственный за регистрацию в ближайшем офисе ОВИР.

Маршруты в Каракалпакстан (Нукус)

Самолеты: Прямые международные рейсы только из Москвы (Россия). Местные рейсы из Ташкента летают два раза в день национальной авиакомпанией Uzbekistan Havo yullari.

Поезда: Поезда из или в Ташкент ездят несколько раз в неделю; существуют прямые стыковки с Москвой, Санкт Петербургом, Саратовом (Россия), Душанбе, Ходжант (Таджикистан) и Алматы (Казахстан).

Автобус: Из Ташкента через Самарканд и Бухару два раза в день. Нет рейсов, которые переезжают границу.

Аэропорт (E5)

Аэропорт расположен в северной части Нукуса на ул. Досназарова примерно в 10 минутах езды от центра города.

Билет на самолёт «Авиакасса» (D8/9, E7)

Иностранцы должны оплачивать билеты наличными в долларах США и должны предоставить также две копии паспорта. Билеты также можно купить и в аэропор-

Opening hours of the main office: Mo-Su 9am-6pm, closed 1-2pm

Bazaar (C8/9)

Nukus's main bazaar, the Oraylik-Bazaar or simply "bazaar", was partly renovated in 2011. A ten-minute walk from the famous Savitsky Collection, it is the centre of daily business, where visitors can find food, clothes, household goods, musical instruments and craftsmen. Sunday is the traditional bazaar day when regional citizens visit the bazaar, so it can be particularly full that day.

The bazaar is open every day from dawn to dusk.

Bus Station
Severnyi Avtovokzal (D2)
Yujnyi Avtovokzal (I15)

There are several bus stations in Nukus. Buses to Chimbay and other northern districts leave from the Severnyi (northern) Avtovoksal. Buses to Turtkul, Urgench, Samarkand and Tashkent leave from Yujnyi (southern) Avtovoksal. Buses to Muynak and Kungrad leave from the train station.

Train station (I14)

The train station is located at

ту. Режим работы главного офиса: С понедельника по воскресенье 09:00 - 18:00.

Базар (C8/9)

Главный базар в Нукусе, Oraylik-базар или просто «базар», был частично реконструирован в 2011 году. Находясь в десяти минутах ходьбы от знаменитого музея Савицкого, базар является центром повседневной жизни, где посетители могут купить продукты питания, одежду, предметы домашнего обихода, музыкальные инструменты и встретить ремесленников. Воскресенье является традиционным днем базара, когда посетители со всей республики приходят на базар, так что базар может быть особенно шумным и полным в этот день. Базар открыт ежедневно от рассвета до заката.

Автостанция
Северный Автовокзал (D2)
Южный Автовокзал (I15)

В Нукусе несколько автостанции. Автобусы до Чимбая и других северных районов выезжают с Северного Автовокзала. Автобусы до Турткуля, Ургенча, Самарканда и Ташкента выезжают с Южного Автовокзала. Автобусы до Муйнака и Кунграда выезжают с железнодорожного вокзала.

Железнодорожный вокзал (I14)

Железнодорожная станция рас-

the southern end of Dosnazarov Street. The schedule is available online on: http://fahrplan.oebb.at/bin/query.exe/en

Opening hours of the counter Mo-Su: 9am-6pm, closed 12am-1pm

Banks/ ATM
Kapital Bank (E7)
Asaka Bank (E9)

There is no ATM in Nukus, but it is possible to draw cash with a VISA card at the Kapital Bank or with MASTER card at the Asaka Bank. If you want to change money, it is necessary to bring your passport and customs declaration.

Opening hours: Mo-Fr: 9am-5pm

Emergency
Police (H11)
Hospital (E7)

Call for fire: 01, police: 02, ambulance: 03. Russian and Karakalpak speaking only.

Gas Station (D6, H13, H15, I14)

Petrol is not always available. Gas is more likely to be found.

Internet (C9, D11, H11)

Internet is available at several hotels. It is also available in internet clubs.

положена в южной части ул. Досназарова. С расписанием можно ознакомиться на английском в Интернете на: http://fahrplan.oebb.at/bin/query.exe/en. Касса работает с понедельника по воскресенье 09:00 - 12:00 и 13:00 - 18:00.

Банки / банкоматы
Kapital Bank (E7)
Asaka Bank (E9)

В Нукусе нет банкоматов, но можно снять наличные в Kapital банке с картой VISA или в Asaka банке с картой MASTER. Если вы хотите разменять деньги, необходимо взять с собой таможенную декларацию. Режим работы: С понедельника по пятницу 09:00 - 17:00.

Аварийный случай
Полиция (H11)
Больница (E7)

Номер Пожарная служба: 01, Полиция: 02, скорая помощь: 03.

Автозаправочная станция (D6, H13, H15, I14)

Бензин не всегда доступен. Газ, скорее всего, легче найти, но желательно, отойти на безопасное расстояние пока машина заправляется.

Интернет (C9, D11, H11)

Интернет доступен в нескольких отелях. Он также доступен в интернет-клубах.

Pharmacy

The Uzbek/ Karakalpak word for pharmacy is "Dorixona", the Russian word is "Apteka" (Аптека).

24/7 pharmacy (E7, F13)

Post office (E9)

The main post office is on Karakalpakstan St. across from the Nukus Hotel. National envelopes are required to send letters and post cards abroad and may be bought at the post office. Opening hours: Mo-Fr: 9am-6pm

Taxi

Taxis are easily available in Nukus, however most drivers don't speak English. Although most street names have changed shortly after the independence, Soviet street names are widely used and are written in brackets in the city map of Nukus.

Tourist Information Centre

There is no Tourist Information Centre in Nukus, but the hotel staff can usually provide you with helpful information about guided tours. More information are available at:

www.karakalpakstan.org
www.karakalpak.com
www.facebook.com/pages/Discover-Karakalpakstan

Аптека

«Dorixona»/ «Darihana» - Узбекское/ каракалпакское слово аптека. Круглосуточная аптека (E7, F13)

Почта (E9)

Главпочтамт находится по ул. Каракалпакстан напротив гостиницы Нукус. Для отправки письма необходимо использовать национальные конверты, которые можно купить в почтамте. Режим работы: С понедельника по пятницу 09:00 - 18:00

Такси

В Нукусе такси можно найти легко, но многие таксисты не разговаривают на Английском. Хотя многие названия улиц поменялись после обретения независимости, но тем не менее советские названия улиц все еще широко используются и в карте города Нукуса указаны в скобках.

Информационный центр для туристов

Нет информационный туристический центр в Нукусе, но персонал отеля могут предоставить вам полезную информацию об экскурсиях. Вы можете найти больше информации на сайтах:

www.karakalpakstan.org
www.karakalpak.com
www.facebook.com/pages/Discover-Karakalpakstan

CONTENT:

Publisher - Marat Akhmedjanov
publisher@ocamagazine.com

Co-publisher - Aleksandra Vlasova
silkroadmedia.copublisher@ocamagazine.com

Editor and Compiler - Anja Weidner
anja.weidner@giz.de

Project manager - Anastacia Lee
silkroadmedia.books@ocamagazine.com

Designer - Viktoriya Rodionova
designer@ocamagazine.com

Authors:
Anja Weidner, Makset Karlibaev, Olivia Schuckert

Photographers:
Peter Navratil, Anastacia Lee, Evelin Kirklionis,
Fabian Loew, Makset Karlibaev, Olivia Schuckert,
Anja Weidner, Azamat Matkarimov, Daniel Hug,
Hannelore Bendsen, Ruth Pester-Hettche,
Hannelore Bendsen, Katrin Schrickel.

Cover photo by
Discovery Karakalpakstan #1

Maps
Viktoriya Rodionova

Materials for Discovery Karakalpakstan travel guide were
prepared in cooperation with GIZ Uzbekistan, www.giz.de

EST. 2002
Silk Road Media

Silk Road Media

Suite 125, 43 Bedford str., Covent Garden,
London, WC2E 9HA
e-mail: publisher@ocamagazine.com
www.silkpress.com,
www.hertfordshirepress.com

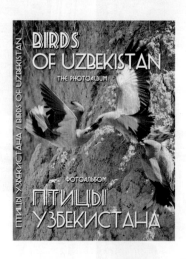

Birds of Uzbekistan
by Roman Kashkarov & Boris Nedosekov

This is a superb collection of full-colour photographs provided by the members of Uzbekistan Society for the Protection of Birds, with text in both English and in Russian.

Since the collapse of the Soviet Union and Uzbekistan's declaration of independence in 1991, unlike in other Central Asian states there have been no such illustrated books published about the birds of this country's rich and diverse wildlife.

There are more than 500 species of birds in Uzbekistan, with 32 included in the International Red Data Book. After independence, Uzbekistan began to attract the attention of foreign tourist companies, and particularly those specialising in ornithological tourism and birdwatching. Birds of Uzbekistan is therefore a much-needed and timely portrait of this element of the country's remarkable wildlife.

ISBN: 978-0955754913
Hardback, English

Available on amazon.com, amazon.co.uk,
www.discovery-bookshop.com

HERTFORDSHIRE PRESS

The aim of the imprint is to publish Central Asian literature
in English in print and electronically for distribution in UK and worldwide,
and to publish English literature in Central Asian languages,
especially for schools and universities in Central Asia.

Promotion of Central Asia in print

01 BANGLADESH

This subcontinental treat might just be the cheapest place on earth to travel. Bangladesh offers marvellous meals for under US$1, a midrange hotel room for less than 10 times that. This means that anyone who isn't a masochist goes up a price bracket or two. You'll pay a little more to get around the Sunderbans National Park on a tiger-spotting tour – US$150 or thereabouts – but it's still peanuts, even compared to what you pay next door in India. Bangladesh is almost disgracefully under-visited. Here, paddleboat is one of the main forms of transport and you can trek, canoe and even surf to your heart's content with some of the world's friendliest people for company.

The Rocket is Bangladesh's most famous ferry, running daily between the capital Dhaka and Khulna. First-class river cruising for 27 hours will cost US$15.

02 NICARAGUA

As other Central American destinations inflate prices with an influx of travellers, there are still a few good-value delights to be found in the region. Nicaragua is somewhere where the careful traveller can get by spending US$15 a day, and midrange comforts can be had for less than double that amount. What you get for your money is nothing short of spectacular: hammock-hanging opportunities on the mythically unspoilt Corn Islands, bar-hopping and live music in colonial León and Granada, and volcano trekking on the Isla de Ometepe.

Paying departure tax when flying out of Nicaragua may be the single most expensive thing you do at US$32, and this is usually already included in the price of your ticket.

03 WASHINGTON, DC, USA

Lincoln Memorial: free. National Air and Space Museum: free. Capitol: free. Library of Congress: free. White House and State Department: tough to get in, but free. Get the picture? Washington is a city packed with iconic things to do and very few of them ask for an entry fee. If you're happy to walk and bring your own lunch bag, you can absorb centuries of American history, politics and culture without having to so much as touch a dollar bill all day.

DC's Kenilworth Park and Aquatic Gardens is the only national park in the USA devoted to water plants. It's free.

✪ PARIS, FRANCE

The French capital is never going to win any awards for cheapness, but here's a winning formula that anyone can afford. First, you need a Swiss Army knife. Then stroll into a *boulangerie* – every neighbourhood has several – and buy a freshly baked baguette for €1 (US$1.35) or thereabouts. Follow your nose to your next stop, a *fromagerie*, and grab a fist-sized hunk of cheese. Lastly, grab a bottle of wine, nothing fancy, and head for the banks of the Seine opposite Notre Dame or the garden adjacent to Pont Neuf on a sunny day, preferably with a loved one. *Zut alors* – a Parisian dining experience for under €10 (US$13.50) per person that any local would declare *formidable!*

You'll find everything for a picnic on Rue Montorgueil in the 2nd arrondisement.

✪ NAMIBIA

Botswana wants big spenders only and South Africa's not the deal it once was, so southern Africa bargain hunters should head for Namibia. Well set-up for backpackers, this is still a territory of US$50 or less a day if you're careful, with an excellent network of local minibuses and tours aimed at budget travellers to go to places public transport won't. And if you go up a price bracket you'll eat and sleep well in excellent-value midrange options that bring South Africans flocking over the border year after year.

Admission to the Cape Cross Seal Reserve on the Skeleton Coast costs a mere US$3 per person.

✪ PHILIPPINES

The Philippines may be just about to rudely shove Thailand off the 'best cheap beaches' perch it's occupied for the best part of two decades. While travellers argue long and hard about which is cheaper, there's no denying Thailand is more popular. For those who desire nothing more than to find great, undiscovered beaches, surf the odd wave and eat unique, distinctive food for under US$20 a day, the Philippines has the edge. Add in the possibility of beach camping along the Zambales Coast or in the Bacuit Archipelago and you've got the recipe for timeless island hopping that suits any budget.

Ferries link many idyllic destinations in the Philippines. Expect to pay around US$5 for each hour you're on the water.

✪ ARGENTINA

The Argentine peso is the currency that keeps on giving. In the middle of the last decade, incredulous visitors regularly queried bills for being too cheap after feasting on fine steak and red wine. While not quite the bargain it was during those years, the country still offers a terrific deal. Characterful midrange hotels start at around AR$180 (US$46) per night in Buenos Aires and Patagonia, and half that in other places. Argentina's gourmet eating houses usually won't charge more than US$30 a head and you can enjoy wonderful meals on much less. Best of all, you get great quality food, wine, lodging and transport throughout Argentina for your money.

Bounce up and down with some of Buenos Aires' more raucous citizens at a fútbol (soccer) match. Terrace tickets for Boca Juniors, River Plate and others cost from AR$14 (US$3.60).

✪ NAPLES, ITALY

Italy: not cheap. Even a slice of pizza can seem like lousy value if you've come from a part of the world that uses a currency that's slumped against the euro. Thank heavens then for Naples. Here's one Italian city that prefers food that's fresh, simple and good value. You can dine brilliantly on the city's spectacular street food alone. Naples eschews budget-blasting frills in favour of small and simple B&Bs charging around €75 (US$100) per night. Best of all,

Naples is a city full of life being lived for its own sake, with few of the tourist hordes who descend on other Italian classics further north.

The ferry from Naples to the idyllic island of Capri, one of Italy's classic journeys, costs a mere €10.50 (US$14) with Caremar (www.caremar.it).

✪ UKRAINE

Eastern Europe isn't the US50c-a-beer haven for bargain hunters it once was, but good deals are still available. OK, midrange hotels can be pricey, especially in the capital, Kyiv, but good budget options in Lviv and Odessa are available for less than US$50. Once on the ground you'll find your funds go a long way. Public transport is fantastic value, with a train between Kyiv and the lovely city of Lviv costing less than US$10, and a tram ride from the station into town a hundredth of that. If you know where to look, food, beer and coffee can be really very cheap.

One of Ukraine's top sights is the immense and moving Lychakiv Cemetery in Lviv; it includes the final resting place of national poet Ivan Franko and thousands of dramatic tombstones. You get hours of fascinating wandering for less than US$1.

✪ SYRIA

While some neighbouring countries up the entry costs to ancient sites, Syria remains an excellent-value place to travel. As you might expect, there are superb street *shwarma* (sandwiches), felafel and eye-tightening *qahwa* (coffee) available for small change. A ride between Aleppo and Damascus won't touch US$5, and a daily budget of US$50 will get you well into the midrange bracket. Best of all, the delights of the Old City of Damascus and the *souq* (market) at Aleppo are free. If you get locked into a tussle with a carpet merchant in the latter, though, you're on your own.

The Crusader Castle of Crac des Chevaliers, one of the world's great castles, charges around US$3.50 entry.

RICHARD I'ANSON » LPI

BANGLADESH – IT'S BUDGET FRIENDLY AND JUST PLAIN FRIENDLY IN GENERAL

THE 10 BEST
THINGS TO DO
IN 2011

PUNCTUATE THIS YEAR WITH MEANINGFUL EXPERIENCES. CHOOSE
FROM OPTIONS THAT GIRDLE THE GLOBE – FROM CRICKET BATS
AND BIRTHDAY PARTIES TO SOBERING MEMORIALS OR A COPY OF
LED ZEPPELIN IV.

01 HUG A TREE IN THE AMAZON

The UN is declaring 2011 the International
Year of the Forest, with events planned
from El Salvador to Bulgaria to help
promote and preserve the globe's forests.
Sounds like a good time for the ultimate
forest, the Amazon. The region, which is
about as broad as the continental USA,
is filled with opportunities, even in the
wake of deforestation. Brazil's main hub
for the Amazon is Manaus, reached by
plane or a five-day boat ride inland from
Belém, where you can book tours to hike
in the jungle, spot dolphins, toucans and
monkeys, fish for piranha, and opt for
luxury cabins on stilts. Try going in June
and July when high tide means 'hikes' are
done by canoe. Trips can also be arranged
from places like Leticia, Colombia or
Iquitos, Peru.
*Brazil's Mamiraué Reserve (www.mamir
aua.org.br), the nation's oldest sustain-
able reserve, really gets 'eco' right – stay
in the floating Pousada Uacari (www.
pousadauacari.com.br) or cabins on
stilts.*

02 CRICKET IN INDIA & SRI LANKA

You can break the ice with locals in India
by talking Bollywood or curry, but why let
the real national pastime take the backseat?
Cricket reigns here above all else, and in
2011 (the 290th anniversary of the first
recorded match in India) it's no contest. In
February and March, India and Sri Lanka
host the Cricket World Cup (India's third
time). India has never won at home – only
winning in England in 1983 – and all eyes
will be on three-peat champions Australia.
Wherever you are, get some makeshift
lessons and connect with locals. And see
if you can't get a seat at Mumbai's newly
renovated Wankhede Stadium for the final.
*To get some pre-trip tingle in your wicket,
check out India's cricketing pulse at www
.cricinfo.com or www.cricbuzz.com. Sri
Lanka's turning the occasion into a broad
Visit Sri Lanka Year.*

03 VISIT THE NEW 9/11 MEMORIAL, NEW YORK CITY

New York's World Trade Center
site has been closed to the public since

CHRISTER FREDRIKSSON » LP

9/11, but on the 10th anniversary of the attacks this September, the National September 11 Memorial opens the site for public viewing for the first time. Construction of nearby towers (including the Freedom Tower) and the memorial's museum will be ongoing, but in the 6-acre plaza, one can view waterfalls lined with the names of all 9/11 victims and get a sneak preview of two recovered 'tridents' (steel columns) from the former WTC that will fill the museum atrium in 2012.

The not-for-profit organisation running the memorial plans to open the museum by 11 September 2012. Get more information at www.national911memorial.org.

✪ DIY WONDERS OF THE WORLD LIST

We do like lists, don't we? The overlap of Ancient Wonders of the World, Wonders of the Underwater World and Wonders of the Industrial World grows in 2011 with the New Wonders of the World's 2nd edition, this time focusing on nature. It's all decided by public vote, with many good candidates including Venezuela's Angel Falls, Argentina/Brazil's Iguazu Falls and Vietnam's Halong Bay. Spend 2011 trying to visit all seven or create your own dang list. Seven Wonders of the Sports World, or maybe Top Seven Smug Politician Failures or Top Seven Places that Stink?

The New Seven Wonders of the World Foundation (www.new7wonders.com) unveils the results of the new list on 11 November 2011.

✪ PAN AMERICAN GAMES, GUADALAJARA, MEXICO

The birthplace of tequila, mariachis and the Mexican broad-rimmed sombrero, Guadalajara is without a doubt a memorable spot to party. It's a nice alternate gateway to Mexico City for accessing nearby colonial towns like San Miguel de Allende and Guanajuato. *And it's set to really let loose from 13 to 30 October when the Western Hemisphere's Olympics – aka Pan American Games – comes knocking. The games, held every four years since 1951, feature 5000 athletes representing 42 countries.*
For information on events and tickets, check the official website of the games,

Guadalajara 2011 (www.guadalajara2011. org.mx).

✪ FIS NORDIC WORLD SKI CHAMPIONSHIPS, OSLO, NORWAY

Nothing beats the flag-waving frenzy of Norwegians cheering on their skiers at any winter event and that only escalates when the event is local. Oslo hosts the FIS Nordic World Ski Championships from 24 February to 6 March, a serious skiing affair of 21 events including the famed Holmenkollen Ski Jump, site of the world's oldest ski jump. At its museum you can learn about the delicate art of ski jumping and skiing's 4000-year history, as well as take a simulated ski jump for a laugh (a queasy laugh anyway).
You can visit Holmenkollen's Ski Museum all year (www.skiforeningen.no); for more on the event check its website www. oslo2011.no.

THERE'S NOTHING STILTED ABOUT THESE LOCALS ON COMBO ISLAND NEAR BELÉM, BRAZIL

✪ CLIMB A 'STAIRWAY TO HEAVEN'

Robert Plant swears the lyrics to the Led Zeppelin's rock anthem 'Stairway to Heaven' (turning 40 on 8 November; long live rock!) were written off the cuff, and that there really aren't Satanic messages in that wonderful 'a bustle in your hedgerow' part when you play it backwards. But with a little imagination you can place the 'stairway' near Bron-Yr-Aur, the Welsh cottage where Jimmy Page first put together the immortal chords. In the south of Snowdonia National Park, the 892m Cader Idris is the big climb here, reached in five hours along the rocky Ty Nant Path or Dolgellau Path – or with stronger thighs via the Minffordd Path. Views up there can make you wonder. *Page's old cottage is near Wales' 'green capital' Centre for Alternative Technology, incidentally home to one of the world's steepest funicular trains. You can arrange tours and stay in ecocabins (www.cat. org.uk).*

✪ ISLE OF MAN TT MOTORBIKE RACE

A haven for tax dodgers and outdoorsy types most of the year, the remote oddball Isle of Man transforms in May and June for the Tourist Trophy, an engine-revving motorbike race that attracts 50,000 people every year – and 2011 is its 100th birthday. You can reach it by plane, or boat from Liverpool, and you can see much of the island by rental bike or on foot; the 95-mile Raad ny Foillan is a complete circuit of the island. Peek at past TT winners at the Manx Museum in the island's main town of Douglas.

Keep up to date with contestants and past TT glory at the race's website (www. iomtt.com).

✪ INDY 500, INDIANAPOLIS, USA

On the subject of engines and 100th birthdays, the USA's premier motor race also turns 100 in 2011. Indianapolis Motor Speedway hosts the event over the Memorial Day weekend in late May, but celebrates the race all month. You can take a bus tour of the 2.5-mile oval track any time – at a snail-like 60km/h (see www.indianapolismotorspeedway.com). *Plan way ahead if you want to join up to 450,000 fans at the actual race. See imstix.com for ticket information.*

✪ WRITE A POSTCARD

E-books, mobile phone apps, augmented reality – we live and travel in a world of instant information and sore thumbs. This year is a good time to pause and revisit that ol' travel chestnut: the postcard. What started a century ago as a craze of keepsakes (recipients cherished them as much as travellers sending them cherished their actual experiences) has lost out to wi-fi, text messaging and Flickr images. A shame. Sending a postcard leads to all sorts of local life commonly missed – stationery shops, post offices, funny stamps – as well as the art of actually writing with a pen.

Of course you can also send a physical postcard digitally. Upload a shot from a mobile phone to HazelMail (www. hazelmail.com), which will print and send it for you.

MOST
SUPER-LUXE
TRAVEL

IF MONEY'S NO OBJECT THERE'S NO SHORTAGE OF WAYS TO SPEND IT. HERE'S OUR RUNDOWN OF THE MOST WALLET-WALLOPING HOLIDAYS AND SOME MUST-HAVE EXTRAS.

01 SINGAPORE AIRLINES' DOUBLE-BED SUITES

When you're engaged in a perpetual battle for the bums of some of the world's richest people on your seats you've got to pull out all the stops. So when Singapore Airlines turned their minds to how to fit out the First Class cabins of their A380 behemoths they hit on a novel idea. Why not blast all arguments about legroom out of the water by creating a double-bed suite, created by a French luxury yacht designer, complete with privacy blinds? One word of warning: if you attempt what the airline terms 'inappropriate activity' you'll be asked, probably very politely, to stop.

Singapore Airlines Suites with double beds are only available on routes served by A380. Fares vary but we were quoted about £4160 (US$6445) per person for a return flight from London to Singapore, so double it. Visit www.singaporeair.com.

02 SUPERCAR HIRE

Sometimes that Toyota Prius with unlimited mileage just isn't enough.

Happily, several companies exist to cater to your needs. Should you dream of roaring round rural English lanes, Dream Car Hire can fix you up with everything from a Ferrari 430 F1 Spider to a Bentley GT Convertible. Around £500 (US$775) a day is what's needed to get you into the serious machinery realm, but that'll be pocket change compared to what you could end up paying in speeding fines. *A Lamborghini Gallardo for three days with 200 miles allowance will cost £2085 at www.dreamcarhire.com.*

03 YOUR OWN DESERT ISLAND

Always dreamed of being a castaway? Island broker Farhad Vladi can help. He rents and sells exclusive island retreats all over the world where the ample-walleted can escape the stresses and strains of everyday life and not have to worry about meeting anyone else. Choose from a Spanish island with a castle on it (sleeps 16, US$2019 per day) or Fiji's Dolphin Island, a tiny coral paradise costing US$6600 for four nights for up to four guests. And if renting's not enough, how about Cornish Cay in the Bahamas, on offer for you to buy outright for a mere US$9 million? Vladi also sells rare editions of *Robinson Crusoe* should you want something to read.

Vladi Private Islands (www.vladi-private-islands.de) can help you if you want to rent, buy or even sell an island. Artificial duckpond islands don't count.

✪ THE MUST-HAVE SUBMARINE

Virgin supremo Richard Branson got into the island-buying game years ago with his purchase of Necker Island, and its exclusive appeal is no secret. His yacht, the Necker Belle, is also available for hire for US$88,000 per week. Doing that will also allow you, for a further US$25,000, to take charge of Necker Nymph, the three-seater submarine for the week. The sub is modelled on a fighter jet and as you use it to explore the clear blue Caribbean seas you can console yourself that it might be expensive, but at least you get to disturb the billionaire tycoon's buttock grooves in the driver's seat.

Necker Island and Necker Belle can both be booked through www.virginlimited edition.com.

✪ GENEVA'S BIGGEST-TICKET HOTEL ROOM

Even by the standards of superlatively priced luxury hotels in Switzerland, a country not celebrated for its value, the Royal Penthouse Suite at Geneva's President Wilson Hotel is pushing it a

HOW HWEE YOUNG/EPA » COREI!

ROOM SERVICE ON A PLANE? DOUBLE-BED SUITES ON THE AIRBUS A380 BRING A WHOLE NEW LEVEL OF LUXURY TO AIR TRAVEL

bit. For a mere US$65,000 a night you get a private lift, a massive suite with unbeatable views over Lake Geneva and a team dedicated to providing you with anything you might conceivably desire. Visiting dignitaries attending pow-wows at the UN or World Economic Forum are the most regular guests.

Perhaps oddly, haggling is the name of the game when booking such a suite. The quoted 'rack rate' is rarely paid. Give the hotel a call on +41 22 906 6666. They'll probably cut you a deal.

✪ SOLID GOLD TRANS-SIBERIAN

Anyone who has squeezed into a four-berth compartment for the week-long ride across Europe and Asia on a Trans-Siberian train, look away now. Billed as the world's most luxurious train ride, the Golden Eagle Trans-Siberian Express will take some beating. Cabins can be up to seven sq metres – that's bigger than many hotel rooms. Some come equipped with underfloor heating and private entertainment systems, and meals are taken in restaurant cars serving top-notch regional cuisine. And unlike the public Trans-Siberian trains there won't be a sozzled Russian soldier trying to ply you with vodka in sight.

Fifteen day Moscow–Vladivostok trips travelling in Gold Class start at US$15,795, booked via GW Travel (www.gwtravel. co.uk).

✪ THE ULTIMATE LUGGAGE

Forget matching Vuitton luggage sets, what sets the discerning traveller apart from the pack is a HENK suitcase. Or, as HENK's motto states 'No suitcase'. Each one is custom-built to unique specifications and boasts retractable wheels, central gravity handle and a capacity of 30L. It also complies with IATA hand luggage restrictions, which is just as well as at around US$20,000 each you wouldn't want it roughly manhandled in the hold.

Have a look at HENK's specifications at www.henk.com.

✪ BEEF BEEFS UP THE BILL

Wine normally tips the cost of a meal from merely being expensive into the 'You what?' category, but Aragawa, in Tokyo's Shinbashi district, relies on its main ingredient, the world's finest Kobe beef. This unassuming steakhouse uses only meat from the seriously pampered Sanda-gyu herd, who during their life have regular massages and are fed beer and, rumour has it, given special treatments by carers to stimulate blood flow. The price tag ensures that only gourmands with deep pockets need try for a table. Two seafood appetisers, a 200g piece of Sanda-gyu sirloin and tea or coffee will set you back US$370 per person.

There's no website, but your hotel concierge is the best person to get you a table at Aragawa. Failing that, try the concierge at a more expensive hotel, and tip them.

✪ THE WORLD'S POSHEST SAFARI

Upmarket safaris have become common currency in recent years, so those aiming to attract the super-rich need to go a step further. Ol Lentille in the foothills of Mt Kenya is four luxury private houses which come with a private butler, your own safari guide and – what else – a dreamy horizon pool overlooking classic African scenery. It's US$750 a night per person in peak season or for US$13,500 six of you can have full run of the sumptuous Chief's House for three nights.

Find out more and book the Sanctuary at Ol Lentille at www.ol-lentille.com.

✪ ASK JEEVES

Sometimes it all gets a bit too much and, with all that money to spend, you need someone to help out with day-to-day life. What you need is a butler, and a professionally trained one at that. The best butlers don't come cheap, but then, as they'll end up travelling the world with you, packing and unpacking your shirts, folding napkins and generally being the soul of discretion, you should be prepared to pay a bit.

The International Guild of Professional Butlers (www.butlersguild.com) can advise you on recruiting the right sort of chap.

HIRE THIS RACY ITALIAN OR ANOTHER SUPERCAR OF YOUR CHOICE FOR A FANTASY GETAWAY

TOP 10 PLACES TO LEARN
HOW TO COOK
THE LOCAL CUISINE

MAKE YOUR POST-TRIP SLIDESHOW TO FRIENDS MORE INTERESTING BY OFFERING A FEW AUTHENTIC RECIPES YOU'VE PICKED UP WHILE ON THE ROAD.

01 LUANG PRABANG, LAOS

Tiny, landlocked Laos is often overshadowed by close neighbours Thailand and Vietnam, but Southeast Asia's most laid-back country also has its own unique and tasty cuisine, especially in the former royal city of Luang Prabang. After rising at dawn to offer alms to saffron-robed monks, learn the secrets of local specialities like *jąew bąwng*, a condiment made with chillies and dried buffalo skin, and *khai phụn*, dried river algae fried with sesame seeds. Both are tastier than they sound, and with a cold Beer Lao, *khai phụn* is one of the world's best bar snacks.

The Tamarind restaurant (www.tamarind laos.com) offers full-day cooking courses in an airy lakeside pavilion. Courses include a visit to the local market.

02 İSTANBUL, TURKEY

The geographic meeting point of Europe and Asia showcases a cuisine influenced by the Ottoman Empire's historic spread far beyond the waters of the Bosphorus. Get inspired in local markets and restaurants crammed with Balkan flavours from the West, and Middle Eastern influences from the East beyond Asia Minor. Feast on excellent street food like *midye tava* (stuffed mussels), or fresh fish sandwiches from the Eminönü docks. Traditional dishes include *yayla çorbasi (*yoghurt soup with mint) and *imam bayıldı* (stuffed eggplant); the latter translates literally to 'the Imam fainted', an allusion to the legendary positive response the iconic dish received when it was first cooked.

Located in an elegant heritage restaurant in Sultanahmet, Cooking Alaturka (www.cookingalaturka.com) runs four-hour courses culminating in a relaxed, shared lunch.

03 OAXACA, MEXICO

The regional cuisine of Oaxaca is proud and passionate proof there's more to Mexican food than nachos and burritos. The city is renowned to food lovers as 'lugar de siete moles' (the place of seven *moles*), and different spins on Oaxaca's signature sauce tinged with chilli and chocolate are available in the city's restaurants and markets. Visit the Abastos market for the local breakfast speciality, *huevos oaxaqueños* – eggs

ANDERS BLOMQVIST » LPI

poached in a chilli-tomato soup – and after a shot of the local mezcal firewater, graduate to chowing down on *chapulines* (roasted grasshoppers). Oaxaca chocolate is also pretty good if insects aren't to your taste.

Cooking classes at Oaxaca's Casa Crespo Bed & Breakfast (www.casacrespo.com), are held in the attached El Teatro Culinario restaurant (www.elteatroculinario.com).

✪ BANKS PENINSULA, NEW ZEALAND

With hiking, swimming with dolphins, and kayaking all on offer, you could visit New Zealand's picturesque Banks Peninsula and easily overlook the region's growing foodie credentials. Visit raffish Lyttelton on a Saturday morning for one of New Zealand's best farmers' markets,

or ask about cooking classes and buy Kiwi craft beers at the Ground Culinary Centre (www.ground.co.nz). Come back on a Sunday to attend the She Chocolate School (www.shechocolat.com) at neighbouring Governor's Bay. Around nearby Akaroa Harbour, the emphasis is on self-exploration, with excellent boutique cheese and wine waiting to be discovered. *Located in the former French colony of Akaroa, the Akaroa Cooking School (www. akaroacooking.co.nz) focuses on local, organic ingredients including lots of fresh New Zealand seafood.*

✪ HOI AN, VIETNAM

Most travellers visit Hoi An to explore the town's colonial history – including Portuguese, French and Japanese influences – or to get a new wardrobe whizzed up by skilled tailors. The sleepy settlement is also a good place to learn to cook Vietnamese food, and local specialities include *cao lau*, a noodle dish influenced by Japanese *soba* noodles. A recommended spin is to scatter crumbled *bánh da* rice crackers on top like Asian-style croutons. Hoi An's riverside night market is one of Vietnam's best, but try to get to bed relatively early so you can explore the town's fish market come daybreak.

Courses at the Red Bridge Restaurant and Cooking School (www.visithoian.com) include visits to local farms and markets.

✪ CHIANG MAI, THAILAND

Thailand's second city – the 'Rose of the North' – may be gradually enshrouding its ancient walled bones under a cloak of Asian modernity, but it's still very easy to escape the bustle at relaxed cookery schools. Before you sign up, pay a visit to the city's famed night markets for a crash course in Sampling Thai Cuisine 101. The city's renowned night bazaar operates every night of the week, and every Sunday night Chiang Mai's Ratchadamnoen Rd is transformed into 'Walking St'. The gates of the *wats* (temples) lining Ratchadamnoen Rd are thrown open to become giant alfresco food centres.

First opened in 1993, the Chiang Mai Thai Cookery School (www.thaicookeryschool. com) includes market visits and courses from one to five days.

✪ TUSCANY, ITALY

'Tuscany' is pretty definitive shorthand for a sunkissed holiday surrounded by good

GREG ELMS » LPI

food and wine. Italy is also the birthplace of the 'Slow Food' movement, and in Tuscan towns and villages, easygoing *trattoria* serve traditional dishes packed with olive oil, pecorino cheese, and fresh sage, rosemary and thyme. Many dishes are based on vegetables including artichokes, asparagus and wild mushrooms, and the cuisine is simple and robust. Cooking schools dot the Tuscan landscape, and the best incorporate rustic farmhouses set in relaxed country locations. Look forward to (slowly) discovering local markets and speciality food producers.

Tutti a Tavola (www.tutti-a-tavola.com) offers one- to four-day classes with accommodation provided in Tuscan stone villas set on local vineyards.

✪ FEZ, MOROCCO

Moroccan cuisine combines Berber, Moorish, Mediterranean and Arab influences to produce dishes including *couscous*, *tajines* and spicy *merguez* sausages. Highlights of Fez include North Africa's most impressive *medina* (walled city), a riot of colour, sights and sounds from several centuries. For authentic local food without the tourist markup, head to the food stalls near the Jardin Public or the markets near the Bab Bou Jeloud, the main entrance to the *medina*. Good luck getting that terracotta *tajine* back home in one piece, and don't leave town without trying a few refreshing mint teas.

Lahcen's Moroccan Cooking (www.fes cooking.com) combines a morning visit to the local souq (market) with classes in a restored riad (traditional Moroccan courtyard home).

✪ SAN SEBASTIÁN, SPAIN

The humble Spanish *tapas* has taken on the world in recent years, but the planet's best approach to snacking and drinking is still best appreciated in its homeland. In the northern city of San Sebastián, the snacks are dubbed *pintxos* (literally 'spikes'), and traditionally include octopus, mushroom, *morcilla* (blood sausage) and anchovies. Wander from bar to bar sampling each location's speciality, and you'll appreciate the gradual evolution of *tapas* to offer more innovative and modern flavours. Anyone for *foie gras* in a parsley sauce?

In San Sebastián, El Txoko del Gourmet (www.eltxokodelgourmet.com) offers courses from two to five days specialising in tapas and cazuelitas (individual dishes baked in clay pots).

✪ GOA, INDIA

Good luck in getting a handle on the different cuisines of a country as large and diverse as India, but a good place to start is in the southwestern state of Goa. Shaped by the era of Portuguese colonial rule, Goan food includes *chouriço* sausages tinged with a zesty *masala* paste, creamy *bebinca* rice pudding and the region's signature dish, spicy *vindalho* curry (exported in a far inferior form as vindaloo across the world). Try them all on the compact balcony at the Hotel Venite looking out on old Panjim's streets, and the next day try crafting your own versions.

Based in a heritage Portuguese house, Branca's Cooking Classes (detroitinstitute@yahoo.com) offer courses specialising in both Goan cuisine and food from other parts of India.

BEST PLACES
TO SEE RED

COMMEMORATE THE 20TH ANNIVERSARY OF THE SOVIET UNION'S COLLAPSE IN 2011 BY VISITING THESE QUIRKY RELICS FROM THE SOVIET ERA.

01 MOSCOW METRO – MOSCOW, RUSSIA

Don't let the ornate chandeliers fool you, most of Moscow's extra-deep subway stations double as stylish boltholes against bomb blasts – they were constructed during the height of the Soviet regime. In fact, many of the stations still hint at their Soviet pasts, like Ploshchad Revolyutsii, which features bronze castings of Red Army soldiers. According to conspiracy theorists a second super-secret subway system – built during Stalin's rule and codenamed 'D-6' by the KGB – exists below the current infrastructure and links together several government strongholds like the Kremlin, the Federal Security Service, an airport and underground bunker through four different rail lines.

A single ride on the metro costs R26 (US$0.90); trains run from 6am to 1am daily.

02 MUSEUM OF SOVIET ARCADE MACHINES – MOSCOW, RUSSIA

This teeny museum, hidden within the suburbs of Moscow, provides wonderful insight into the more playful side of life under the hammer and sickle. You'll be treated to such riveting throwbacks as 'Repka', a game that recreates the thrilling act of pulling a stubborn turnip out of the earth (to test one's strength). Or you can try your hand at one of the war simulation games like 'Snaiper' and 'Air Fight'. You'll find a retrofitted soda water dispenser for when you work up a sweat, but if you're looking for a scoreboard you'll be sorely disappointed – individual achievement wasn't recognised in Communist Russia... *Swing by and try out your gaming skills on Wednesday evenings or weekend afternoons. See www.15kop.ru/en for details.*

03 THE GREENBRIER – WHITE SULPHUR SPRINGS, WEST VIRGINIA, USA

Fearing the wrath of the missile-wielding Soviets, the US government sprung into action in the late '50s and commissioned 'Project Greek Island' on the grounds of an ultra-swank hotel. It appeared as though the estate was merely adding another wing of rooms, but this was a clever cover-up for the construction of a massive emergency relocation centre underground. The 110,000-sq-ft bunker was meant to house the American Congress during a nuclear attack, and

TOM COCKREM » LPI

featured living quarters, a hospital and a broadcast centre with a phoney backdrop of the Capitol. After the collapse of the Soviet Union, all was revealed in the *Washington Post*.

Daily 90-minute tours of the relocation bunker are on offer for US$30. See www.greenbrier.com/bunker to make reservations.

✪ THE DIEFENBUNKER – CARP, ONTARIO, CANADA

Americans weren't the only ones to take budget-draining measures to safeguard their citizens (namely political leaders) against possible nuclear attacks. In Canada, the government set up a constellation of disaster-proof 'diefenbunkers' (named for John Diefenbaker, the former prime minister who commissioned their construction)

across the nation. The largest one, just a few kilometres beyond the nation's capital, measures over 100,000 sq ft and contains a radio station, an expansive ops centre and a giant vault to store the Bank of Canada's entire gold bar supply. Today, spirited tour guides lead visitors through the city-sized shelter, which is now known as Canada's Cold War Museum.

Tours costing C$14 (US$14) are available year-round. Check out www.diefenbunker .ca for additional details.

✪ KAROSTA PRISON – LIEPAJA, LATVIA

If you're craving some serious punishment, or just want to brag that you've spent the night in a Soviet jail, then sign up to become a detainee for an evening at grungy Karosta Prison, a former detention facility for disobedient

PEEK BEHIND THE FACADE OF THE GREENBRIER RESORT IN WHITE SULPHUR SPRINGS, USA

ANDRE JENNY » ALAMY

soldiers. You'll be subjected to regular bed checks, verbal abuse by guards in period garb and forced to relieve yourself in the world's most disgusting latrine (seriously). Try booking the night in cell 26 – solitary confinement – you won't be bothered, but the pitch-blackness will undoubtedly drive you off the edge. Those only wanting a pinch of masochism can visit the facility on a guided tour. *Sleepover torture sessions and guided tours (noon to 5pm) are available daily between May and September. Dial +371 2636 9470 for reservations.*

✪ MUSEUM OF EROTICA – ST PETERSBURG, RUSSIA

Time and time again those scintillating Soviet sweethearts knew how to catch the wandering eye of the lustful James

Bond, and the Museum of Erotica sheds a bit more light on the subject. Housed in a prostatology clinic, the titillating exhibit features over 10,000 toys and statues of a sexual nature, but the most famous item on display is Rasputin's legendary manhood, snatched up by the Soviets when they seized power. The museum's curator (and head prostatologist) likes to brag that Rasputin left behind a much greater endowment than Napoleon… *Admission to the exhibition space is free for clinic patients; visitors are encouraged to purchase a thematic souvenir (including how-to sex tapes in Russian).*

✪ SOVIET SCULPTURES – MINSK, BELARUS

After the collapse of the Soviet Union, liberated locals began tearing down the looming statues of their deposed despots. But in Belarus, Soviet ideals are still alive and kickin'! In fact, most sculpted homages to commanding comrades still stand tall amongst the city's streets. A stroll through the city centre is like stepping through a time machine: Lenin proudly perches over a podium in front of the House of Government, the bust of Felix Dzerzhinsky, founder of the KGB, watches over pedestrians along Independence Ave, and Mikhail Kalinin, noted Soviet revolutionary, stands guard in his eponymous square.

If you're visiting Belarus, make sure to apply for your tourist visa at least two weeks ahead of time to avoid any logistical snags.

✪ OUTER SPACE

Sure, you'll need, oh, upwards of US$20 million in pocket change to hitch a ride to the stars, but we cannot think of a better throwback to Space Race times. Due to the cost-prohibitive nature of the endeavour, only the Russian Space Agency is currently authorising transport aboard their Soyuz-class spacecrafts; a design which was inaugurated in the 1960s when Soviet cosmonauts were bested by the moon-landing Americans. Today, tourist missions have temporarily been put on hold, but Richard Branson's Virgin Galactic looks to be starting up soon and may give the Russians a run for their money once again...

Check out www.virgingalactic.com for updated information about booking your very own space flight.

✪ THE PENSION – LĪGATNE, LATVIA

Tucked deep within the pines of Gauja National Park is a dreary rehabilitation centre. But this is no ordinary hospital; beneath the bland '60s architecture lies a top-secret Soviet bunker, known by its code name; the Pension. When Latvia was part of the USSR, the Pension was one of the most important strategic hideouts during a time of nuclear threat. In fact, the bunker's location was so tightly guarded that it remained classified information until 2003. Today, visitors can wander through the bunker's iron-clad halls – the 2000-sq-metre shelter still looks as it did when it was in operation some 40 years ago.

To organise your 2Ls (US$3.85) visit of the Pension, check out www.rehcentrs ligatne.lv.

✪ MINSK WORLD – SHENZHEN, CHINA

Like a bizarre Russified Disney floating inexplicably in the South China Sea, Minsk World's main attraction is a restored Soviet aircraft carrier that was once a part of the Pacific fleet. Tourists can clamber around the rusting retro equipment, such as old-school rocket launchers and decommissioned helicopters. Guides clad in slick period attire lead visitors through four floors of gadget-filled rooms until they reach the *pièce de résistance* on the top deck – a mini fleet of decaying MiGs. If you're lucky enough to visit on national holidays, you'll be treated to elaborate military parades.

For more information about Minsk World, visit www.szminsk.com.

TOP 10 COUNTRIES
THAT DIDN'T EXIST
20 YEARS AGO

TURBO BOOST YOUR PASSPORT BY VENTURING TO THESE
RECENTLY MINTED DESTINATIONS. IT'S ALSO A GOOD CHANCE TO
IMPROVE YOUR COLLECTION OF MINIATURE NATIONAL FLAGS.

01 CZECH REPUBLIC

Following Czechoslovakia's
Velvet Revolution in 1989, the Czech
Republic and Slovakia finally sealed
their Velvet Divorce in 1993. Less than
20 years on, Prague neighbourhoods
like elegant Vinohrady and energetic
Žižkov are buzzing, and a country full of
emerging microbreweries proves there's
more to Czech beer than Pilsner Urquell
or Budvar. Add virtue to these delicious
liquid vices by cycling and hiking through
the idiosyncratic landscapes of Bohemian
Switzerland or the Český ráj region. Away
from bustling Prague, discover quieter
provincial gems like Olomouc, Telč and
Loket, all still retaining the essence of
Bohemian and Moravian culture.
Explore the Czech Republic's rapidly ex-
panding beer scene at Prague's Czech Beer
Festival (www.ceskypivnifestival.cz) or the
Olomouc Beer Fest (www.beerfest.cz).

02 EAST TIMOR

The 21st-century's newest nation
finally achieved independence in 2002, 27
strife-torn and tragic years after initially
declaring independence from Indonesia

in 1975. Look forward to basic roads and
infrastructure, but be rewarded with an
intensely warm welcome from the locals.
The easygoing capital Dili is a hub for
thirsty UN and NGO staff looking for new
drinking buddies, and across on sleepy
Atauro Island (www.atauroisland.com),
a fledgling ecotourism scene supports
hiking and diving. Explore East Timor's
Portuguese heritage amid the faded
colonial architecture of Baucau, and check
travel advisories on the country's security
situation before leaving home.
A 30-day travel permit (US$30) is issued to
most nationalities on arrival at Dili airport.
See the Immigration Department of Timor-
Leste (http://migracao.gov.tl/) for the latest.

03 ERITREA

How far would you go for a
really, really good coffee? What if it
was a superb *macchiato* served in an
art deco cafe in an exotic country in the
Horn of Africa? An addictive combination
of sleepy African vibes and an Italian
colonial past also showcases cubist,
expressionist and futurist architecture in
the Eritrean capital of Asmara. In nearby

Massawa, centuries-old Islamic buildings linger in narrow, labyrinthine streets, and the port is the departure point to diving amid Red Sea corals in the Dahlak Archipelago. At the time of writing Eritrea was at war with Ethiopia and some travel restrictions were in place – check travel advisories carefully.

Visas are required by all visitors and should be obtained in advance from an Eritrean embassy or consulate before entering Asmara.

✪ SLOVAKIA

In a region crammed with dramatic castles, Slovakia's Spiš Castle trumps most with an audacious hilltop location and craggy towers and gloomy dungeons straight from a Hammer horror flick. Visit in summer for a full program of events including concerts and mock battles. Following Slovakia's independence in 1993, Bratislava seems in no hurry to become a bustling Central European metropolis, and the cool cafes and bars of the Slovakian capital's beautifully preserved old town are still largely tourist free – take that Prague! Look forward also to being continuously surprised by the funky street art lurking around every corner.

Get active in the High Tatras National Park (www.tanap.sk) before dissolving your weary limbs into Piešťany's healing spa waters (www.spapiestany.sk).

✪ PALAU

How many jellyfish is just enough? How about 10 million, especially when you're swimming with them in Palau's renowned Jellyfish Lake? (Don't worry,

ADORNED IN WHITE, LOCAL WOMEN GATHER FOR THE FESTIVAL OF TIMKAT IN ASSAB, ERITREA

FRANCES LINZEE GORDON » LPI

the local species have evolved with an absence of stingers). With a population of just 20,000, one of the world's newest countries is also one of the smallest. The tiny island nation of Palau showcases some of the Pacific's best diving opportunities with more than 60 vertical drop-offs punctuating locations like Blue Corner, Shark City and Turtle Cove. In 2001, the Palau Shark Sanctuary (www. sharksanctuary.com) was established to further protect Palau's sharks from the Asian shark-fin industry.

As Palau only achieved independence from United States trusteeship in 1994, you'll need to come equipped with US dollars.

✪ SERBIA

Following the dissolution of Yugoslavia from 1990, Serbia has been less open to travellers than neighbouring Croatia or nearby Slovenia. Now Belgrade's gritty cityscape and Europe's most energetic nightlife scene are attracting a vanguard of curious expat residents and intrepid visitors. It's probably your best chance to experience what Prague was like following the fall of communism in 1989. Other essential musical thrills include the annual Exit Festival (www.exitfest.org) – recent acts have included the Chemical Brothers, Patti Smith and Kraftwerk – and the wildly frantic Guča Festival (www.guca.rs), drawing 600,000 visitors annually for the best in manic Roma (gypsy) trumpet playing.

Check out the Belgrade Foreign Visitors Club (www.belgradefvc.com) for the latest expat-informed lowdown on the Serbian capital.

✪ BOSNIA & HERCEGOVINA

For centuries Sarajevo was on the fault line of religion, culture and history, and in today's capital of Bosnia & Hercegovina, mosques, churches and synagogues all huddle beside each other and the Neretva River. The city has emerged from the dark days of the siege of Sarajevo from 1992 to 1996 as an inclusive and collaborative centre for the arts. The annual summer festival Nights of Baščaršija (www. bascarsijskenoci.ba) showcases music, art and dance in Sarajevo's compact Ottoman quarter, and the Sarajevo Film Festival (www.sff.ba) is one of Europe's most important. Poignant memories of the Balkan Wars include Mostar's reconstructed bridge.

Bosnia & Hercegovina is an emerging adventure-tourism destination, with excellent whitewater rafting on the Una and Neretva rivers. See www.greenvisions.ba.

✪ KAZAKHSTAN

Was the inaccurate depiction of Kazakhstan by *Borat* a few years ago a blessing or a curse? The film certainly lifted brand awareness for the Central Asian republic made independent from Moscow in December 1991, but the planet's ninth-largest country remains a mystery to most. Fuelled by revenues from copious oil and gas reserves, Almaty and Astana have emerged as modern-day boomtowns from the Central Asian steppe, but Kazakhs' nomadic roots are still celebrated with one of the world's more...er...interesting cuisines. How does *beshbarmak* (an offal stew) and horsemeat sausage washed down with a shot of vodka sound?

Celebrate the coming of spring with dancing, Kazakh food and equestrian events at the festival of Nauryz in late March.

○ MONTENEGRO

The denouement of the inevitable dissolution of Yugoslavia came in June 2006 when the citizens of tiny Montenegro voted to separate from the federation of Serbia & Montenegro. Despite Montenegro being the smallest piece of the Balkans jigsaw, the rugged country packs in a geography textbook of natural features and spectacles. The country's eponymous 'Black Mountains' cradle the perfect medieval town at Kotor, and the pine-scented Tara River is Europe's deepest canyon and a growing location for river rafting. The tiny island of Sveti Stefan, irredeemably picturesque and joined to the mainland by a slender isthmus, is rapidly regaining its pre–Balkan Wars status as one of Europe's most exclusive destinations.

Passionate twitchers (birdwatchers) should pack their high-powered binoculars for Lake Skadar, one of Europe's most important bird sanctuaries.

○ KOSOVO

Consider the evidence. Kosovo declared unilateral independence from Serbia in 2008, but Kosovo's closest neighbour refuses to accept the declaration. China and Russia agree with Serbia, but almost 70 other nations including the US, Germany and the UK accept Kosovo as an independent state. Membership of the World Bank and the IMF are a given, but UN membership remains elusive due to the veto-trumping machinations of the Security Council. The presence of the UN and NGOs keeps accommodation prices relatively high, so this is definitely one for the true country collectors out there.
In the Kosovar capital of Pristina, visit Bill Clinton Blvd, complete with a giant billboard of the former US president.

JOHN SONES » LPI

THERE'S A NEW WINDOW ON THE WORLD FOR THESE CITIZENS OF THE YOUNG NATION OF EAST TIMOR

BEST PLACES FOR DANCE FEVER

LEAVE THE WALLFLOWERS BEHIND AND LEARN FROM THE PROFESSIONALS IN THESE HOMETOWNS OF HIGH-ENERGY DANCES.

01 FLAMENCO, ANDALUCÍA, SPAIN

Few parts of Europe are as romantic as Andalucía, with its mountains and whitewashed villages, and the Spanish region is also home to one of the most beguiling dances. Flamenco conjures up images of olive-skinned beauties swirling to a percussively played guitar, clicking castanets and clapping. In cities such as Seville, Cádiz and Granada, you can learn how to flick your ruffled dress like a proud *senorita* or stomp your feet like a Córdoban hat-wearing hunk. The schools cater to all levels of interest – from flamenco fanatics to travellers who are equally interested in sampling the local *jamón* (ham).
Don't miss Granada's famous Moorish fortress, the Alhambra. Seville's Feria de Abril (spring fair) begins two weeks after Semana Santa (Easter holy week).

02 TANGO, BUENOS AIRES, ARGENTINA

Argentina is justifiably beloved for its mix of old-world melancholy and Latin passion, and the national dance form is certainly no exception. Tango originated in the working-class neighbourhoods of the Argentinean capital, which is a great place to learn some dance steps. With Buenos Aires' *porteños* (residents) cruising along the city's avenues during the day, most classes take place in the evening. Follow the accordion music to a *milonga* (tango venue or event) to learn moves including the *giro* (turn) and *ocho* (figure eight traced with the feet). There are usually dozens on offer, catering to the throngs of dance-loving *milongueros*. *Buenos Aires' Tango Festival and World Cup (www.tangobuenosaires.gov.ar) takes place in August; the City Dance Championship is in May.*

03 BREAKDANCE, NEW YORK, USA

In the 30-plus years since the Big Apple's b-boys broke out the first hip hop moves, breakdance has entered the mainstream and courses have started. Many classes are geared towards locals rather than tourists, although the NYC Hip Hop Dance Company (www.nyhiphop101.com) welcomes walk-ins at its weekly lessons near Times Sq. It takes a lot of practice and press-ups to master the key manoeuvres – toprock, downrock, power moves, freezes and suicides – but what a city to study the art of breaking. Nightly inspiration is found in the clubs, where you might see legs and arms flying in a breakdance battle.

Explore NYC's hip hop history with a Hush tour (www.hushhiphoptours.com) or lunch at Queens' Hollis Famous Burgers and Hip Hop Museum.

✪ CAPOEIRA, BAHIA, BRAZIL

Capoeira has spread around the world from northeast Brazil, where African slaves developed the fusion of dance and martial arts, but Bahia remains its heartland. Workshops, run by capoeira *mestres* (masters) in state capital Salvador da Bahia, are just one way the city is keeping its Afro-Brazilian heritage alive. Capoeira circles form on the plazas at night, and the action intensifies during festivals, when the colonial buildings are a backdrop for frenzied drum circles. If the martial arts aspect sounds off-putting, don't worry as the sparring is generally playful and little physical contact is involved.

Salvador da Bahia (often shortened to plain old Bahia) is connected to Rio de Janeiro, some 1300km southwest, by bus and plane.

✪ HULA, HAWAII, USA

As if anyone needed another reason to go to Hawaii, the home of atolls, coral reefs, beaches and sunworshippers, it's also the birthplace of hula. Popular culture is full of saccharine images of island princesses swaying beneath the palms, but hula began as an accompaniment to chants containing oral history. At a *halau hula* (school), a *kumu hula* (teacher) will instruct you in the Polynesian dance form's various moves, which symbolise aspects of Hawaiian life such as ocean voyages and volcanic eruptions. Though many

BRUCE BI » LPI

male visitors may be reluctant to wear a loincloth, hula is also performed by men. *Hawaiian hula events include the Merrie Monarch Festival (www.merriemonarch festival.org) in April and the World Invitational Hula Festival (http://worldhula.com) in November.*

✪ WALTZ, VIENNA, AUSTRIA

Developed by Austrian and Bavarian peasants and picked up by the Habsburg royals before spreading to France and beyond, waltz remains important in Vienna during its ball season. If you feel like donning a ballgown or tailcoat and dancing this sensual style of ballroom dance, the season's fixtures include the lavish Opera Ball in the 19th-century Opera House. Fear not, novices don't have to humiliate themselves in front of Austrian society. Schools offer tuition to individuals and couples who want to learn to dance in three-quarter time. The fabulous classrooms include the Pallavicini Palace, where Mozart and Beethoven performed, and a baroque hall. *There's a list of dance classes in Vienna at http://tinyurl.com/yjezwep. The ball season starts on New Year's Eve and runs for three months.*

✪ CEILIDH, EDINBURGH, SCOTLAND

Most people have a brush with *ceilidh* dancing at some point in their life; whether the wedding's taking place among the heather in Scotland, or far away in the Celtic culture–loving New World. The partner-swinging dance began at social gatherings in Scotland and Ireland, so what better place for some coaching than the picturesque Scottish capital. Not only does Edinburgh boast a castle on a volcanic mound, but there are dance classes and *ceilidhs* for all levels of experience. In fact, *ceilidhs* are by definition welcoming, sociable affairs, and even the clumsiest of novices are normally encouraged to try their first reel. *Dance Base (www.dancebase.co.uk) offers drop-in beginners' classes at the Grassmarket; Visit Scotland has a list of upcoming ceilidhs at www.edinburgh. org/events.*

✪ SALSA, CUBA

Forget cigars and Che Guevara. Salsa, a sizzling mix of Latin and Afro-Caribbean rhythms, perfectly encapsulates sultry, multicultural Cuba. It's a sexy, hip-shaking dance, and teachers on the island happily show beginners how to move to the Cuban beat. The internet is awash with two-week, all-inclusive salsa packages, but, if you want some time to cruise in a clapped-out Buick, shorter courses are also available. When it's time to show off your skills, or to pick up some free tips, hit Havana's nightspots with a friend. There are usually half a dozen salsa nights happening; ask your hotel concierge or another local. *Cuba's alluring spots include Santa Clara, dedicated to all things Che, Havana's waterfront and Baracoa, a windswept town on the Atlantic coast.*

✪ BELLY DANCE, İSTANBUL, TURKEY

Exuding all the exoticism of the Middle East, belly dance has fascinated the West ever since Turkey was the centre of the

Ottoman Empire. A fun place to learn the shimmying dance is the city where the Middle East meets Europe, and the Ottomans built palaces: İstanbul. Although many performances are touristy, *göbek dans* (belly dance) goes back centuries in Turkey, where it is more energetic and playful than in countries such as Egypt. Serious instruction is available.

There's a list of teachers at www.belly danceclasses.net/turkey; a recommended company is Les Arts Turcs (www.lesarts turcs.com), which offers private lessons.

✪ MANDINKA DANCE, WEST AFRICA

Wielding instruments such as the *kora* (21-stringed harp) and *djembe* drum,

West Africa's *griots*, the descendents of court musicians, rightfully sit at the forefront of world music. While visiting the region to see, say, Toumani Diabaté play in Bamako, Mali would be remarkable enough, you can also learn to groove like the folk at the clubs and festivals. A cultural or community centre is a good place to find a teacher who can show you some traditional Mandinka dances, which involve a lot of drama and rituals. Outfits such as Senegal's Jamo Jamo Arts (http://jamojamoarts.com) also run dance-focused trips.

Arguably the best West African dancing destinations are Senegal, with Dakar and its Atlantic coastline, and Mali, for the Sahara, River Niger and Bamako.

LOUIS GALLI » ALAMY

BREAK IT DOWN WITH A BREAKDANCING CLASS IN NEW YORK CITY

WORLD'S GREATEST
BOOKSHOPS

THE BEST SPOTS TO BROWSE, BUY, HANG OUT, FIND SANCTUARY AMONG THE SHELVES, RAVE ABOUT YOUR FAVOURITE WRITERS AND MEET BOOK-LOVING CHARACTERS.

01 CITY LIGHTS BOOKS, SAN FRANCISCO, USA

Lawrence Ferlinghetti's City Lights Books is still one of the world's coolest bookshops, almost 60 years after it opened for bohemian business. Having been a meeting point for American literary icons, from beat writers like Jack Kerouac and Allen Ginsberg onwards, it's still central to the city's vibrant cultural scene. As well as two floors of tomes, including those published by City Lights, the shop offers weekly readings and events. More than the nearby Beat Museum, this is the place to feel the boho buzz that once inspired Kerouac *et al* to drive across America to the Bay Area.
Check www.citylights.com for details of upcoming events; and you can do that pretty much anywhere in wi-fi-blanketed San Francisco.

02 LIBRERÍA EL ATENEO GRAND SPLENDID, BUENOS AIRES, ARGENTINA

It's grand, it's splendid and it's a strong contender to be the world's most beautiful bookshop. Occupying a 1920s theatre in downtown BA, El Ateneo has kept the sumptuous auditorium's original furnishings – and added books. Beneath the painted ceiling, shelves have been built into the spectator balconies. When you've finished gawping at the ornate carvings and it's time to put finger to page, the former theatre boxes are now intimate reading rooms. There's a cafe on the stage, between red velvet curtains, and the final firework in the literary spectacle is the round-the-clock opening hours.
Librería El Ateneo Grand Splendid is located on the south side of Ave Santa Fe, 50m west of Ave Callao.

03 LIVRARIA LELLO, PORTO, PORTUGAL

A little over 100 years old, this art nouveau gem in Portugal's second city remains one of the world's most stunning shops – perhaps of any kind. Competing for attention with the books are wrap-around, neo-Gothic shelves, featuring panels carved with Portuguese literary figures. A track, used by the staff for transporting stock in a cart, leads from the entrance to the lolloping red staircase, which winds up to the first floor like an exotic flower. Books are available in English as well as Portuguese, and there's

ANDERS BLOMQVIST » LPI

a small cafe upstairs beneath the stained-glass skylight.

You can continue the art nouveau tour of Porto at Café Majestic and streets such as Rua Galeria de Paris.

✪ SHAKESPEARE & COMPANY, PARIS, FRANCE

Where did the American beat poets go to share cigarettes and profundities when they were in Europe? Shakespeare & Company of course – located in Paris' Latin Quarter, a tome's throw from Notre Dame Cathedral. George Whitman, the eccentric American bibliophile who opened the cosy store in 1951, has handed the reins to his daughter as he approaches 100. Nonetheless, much of Shakespeare & Co's creative, chaotic spirit remains. It's still a prime spot to fill your rucksack with paperbacks, hang with the Left Bank literati, and admire the packed shelves, wooden beams and poetic posters.

Nearby transport links include St-Michel (metro line 4) and St-Michel Notre Dame (RER lines B and C). Visit http://shakespeare andcompany.com for more information.

✪ DAUNT BOOKS, LONDON, UK

London is an armchair explorer's dream, offering high-quality, travel-focused book dens such as Stanford's and The Travel Bookshop. Our favourite is Daunt Books. The mini-chain stocks a lot more than guides and maps, and everything – from biographies to fiction – is handily arranged by country. The green Daunt Books sign is found in five well-heeled enclaves of London, but the Marylebone branch is the original and best. Occupying an Edwardian bookshop, its long oak galleries with polished floors and shelves, graceful skylights and William Morris prints create a peaceful atmosphere. The perfect place for some serious browsing.

The branches at 83 Marylebone High St, Chelsea, Holland Park, Hampstead and Belsize Park open seven days a week; visit www.dauntbooks.co.uk.

✪ ANOTHER COUNTRY, BERLIN, GERMANY

The commendably eccentric Another Country is a hub for everyone from Berlin's expat community to indie bands. The Kreuzberg institution is more of a library than a conventional bookshop; you can pay for the book, return it when you've read it, and get your money back – minus €1.50. In addition to some 20,000 books, the sprawling shop-cum-club offers much-loved events, including the Tuesday night film club, Thursday TV night and Friday dinner. In the finest tradition of leftfield bookstores, Another

Country inspires as well as sells creative efforts, and its website features a comic and a story about the shop.

Located at Riemannstrasse 7, Another Country (www.anothercountry.de) is open Tuesday to Friday 11am to 8pm and weekends from noon to 4pm. The film and TV nights start at 8pm; the dinner at 9pm.

✪ THE BOOKWORM, BEIJING, CHINA

The Bookworm does everything a good bookshop should do – which is a lot more than sell books. The Beijing mothership, which has spawned branches in Suzhuo and Chengdu, has played a huge role in promoting both local and foreign literature. Not only is it one of the few places in China where you can pick up books which are banned in the country,

KRZYSZTOF DYDYNSKI » LPI

BOOKS ARE THE STAR ATTRACTION AT LIBRERÍA EL ATENEO GRAND SPLENDID, BUENOS AIRES, ARGENTINA

it has a lending library with 16,000-plus titles. The library is also the setting for a healthy program of events, from gigs to an annual literary festival. There's even a whisky bar and monthly wine club.
The Bookworm International Literary Festival takes place in Beijing, Suzhuo and Chengdu over two weeks in mid-March; see www.chinabookworm.com.

✪ SELEXYZ DOMINICANEN, MAASTRICHT, THE NETHERLANDS
Occupying a 13th-century Dominican church – which the Dutch city's cyclists had appropriated for bike storage – Selexyz Dominicanen consists of a steel bookstack rising towards the heavens. Cunningly, this both leaves the nave's grandeur intact and creates 1,200 sq metres of selling space – despite the 750-sq-metre floor area. Staircases and a lift lead to the top of the three-storey stack, where you can eyeball 14th-century ceiling paintings. The altar has been superseded by a cafe, with a halo of lights hanging above a cruciform table. It's an award-winning architectural triumph and a peaceful haven for page thumbing.
Close to both Liège in Belgium and Aachen in Germany, Maastricht is connected to Amsterdam, some 220km northwest, by train.

✪ BOOKÀBAR, ROME, ITALY
Just the thought of big, sexy art books makes us consider diverting our travel dollars to collecting coffee table beauties. Alright, it's rash talk; but even hardened travellers might agree when they ogle

the arty tomes in Bookàbar – the perfect setting. With a curvy ceiling and long, smooth shelves, the shop's coolly contemporary, snow-white interior hordes books, catalogues, CDs, DVDs and merchandise. It looks like a space station staffed by extremely well-read astronauts. The neighbours certainly don't lower the tone, as it's part of the Palazzo delle Esposizioni exhibition centre. Bookàbar's adjoining cafe serves dishes inspired by the centre's exhibitions.
Palazzo delle Esposizioni, which normally has a few exhibitions covering various art forms, is near the junction of Via Nazionale and Via Milano.

✪ ATLANTIS BOOKS, SANTORINI, GREECE
In an age when independent bookshops are being replaced by chains and websites, a gang of American and European university graduates realised the dream of opening one – on a Greek island. 'We found an empty building facing the sunset, drank some whiskey and signed a lease,' explains www.atlantisbooks.org, though we suspect it was more of a mission than that. The shop occupies the basement of a whitewashed, cliff-top villa, which the communally minded staff also call home. The terrace overlooking the Aegean hosts cultural happenings, and inside are more cult novels and quality books than you can shake a quill at.
Santorini is linked to Athens by Blue Star Ferries, Hellas Flying Dolphins ferries, Olympic Air and Aegean Airlines.

BEST SECRET ISLANDS

SIX SEASONS OF *LOST* HAVE PROBABLY TAKEN SOME OF THE GLOSS OFF THE ROBINSON CRUSOE EXPERIENCE, SO HERE'S A LIST TO REIGNITE YOUR LOVE AFFAIR WITH DESERT ISLANDS.

01 SOCOTRA, YEMEN

You just have to be intrigued by a destination that describes itself as 'the most alien-looking place on earth'. Ripped from the coast of Gondwanaland by plate tectonics, the four desert islands that form the Socotra group are a treasure-house of biodiversity, with thousands of plant and animal species found nowhere else on earth. Topping the weird list are the barrel-trunked cucumber tree and the dragon's blood tree, which oozes blood-red sap. Despite being closer to Africa than the Arabian Peninsula, Socotra is administered by Yemen, which keeps the islands off the tourist radar.
Modern-day Sinbads can fly to the tiny capital, Hadibu, from Sana'a and Aden with Yemenia Airlines (www.yemenia. com).

02 TORRES STRAIT ISLANDS, AUSTRALIA

As far as you can go in Oz without falling off the map, the Torres Strait Islands are Australia as it might have been if Europeans had never arrived. Spilling north from the tip of Cape York, the 274 islands in the Torres Strait preserve a unique tribal culture that bridges the divide between Aboriginal Australia and Papua New Guinea. The Great Barrier Reef is right on the doorstop and there are airstrips and hotels on Thursday Island and Horn Island, but access to other islands is at the discretion of local tribal councils.
Permits to visit outlying islands must be obtained at least one month in advance from the Torres Strait Regional Authority (www.tsra.gov.au).

03 YAEYAMA ISLANDS, JAPAN

If Godzilla should ever rise from the sea to destroy Tokyo and Osaka, there's only one place to ride out the storm – the idyllic Yaeyama Islands, tucked away at the very southern tip of the Japanese archipelago. Looking more like the Caribbean, the islands of Iriomote, Taketomi and Ishigaki serve up generous portions of sun, sea, sand and sushi. Ishigaki has the best of the beaches, while Taketomi is famous for its traditional Ryukyuan houses and Iriomote is a jungle playground with an open-air *onsen* (hot springs).
Japan Transocean Air (www.jal.co.jp/jta) flies daily from Tokyo to Ishigaki, which is connected to the other islands by regular ferries.

☻ ÎLES DU SALUT, FRENCH GUIANA

Most people have heard of Devil's Island, but few would be able to stick a pin on a map. The smallest of the three Îles du Salut, this infamous former penal colony is separated from the coast of French Guiana by 11km of treacherous, shark-infested waters. Steve McQueen tried to escape the islands repeatedly in *Papillon*, but most modern visitors are willing castaways, lured here by waving palms, chattering macaws and spooky ruins from the penal colony days.

Access to the Îles du Salut is by catamaran from Kourou and the only place to stay is the clubhouse-style Auberge des Iles (www.ilesdusalut.com).

OLIVER STREWE » LPI

HEAD STRAIGHT TO THE TORRES STRAIT IN AUSTRALIA FOR A DESERT ISLAND EXPERIENCE

✪ ULLEUNGDO, SOUTH KOREA

It's easy to see the appeal of tiny Ulleungdo. Midway between South Korea and Japan, this rugged volcanic island is said to have no pollution, no thieves and no snakes – in other words, this is perfect hiking country. Ferries run daily from the mainland to the tiny port at Dodong-ri, where trails climb to the rocky summit of Seonginbong Peak (984m). If you want to really push the boat out, continue to the Dokdo islands – a tiny collection of outcrops that are hotly disputed between Japan and South Korea.

Perched beneath a towering cliff wall, Chusan Ilga Pension (www.chusanilga. com) offers comfortable but satisfyingly rustic accommodation on the rugged north coast.

✪ SAN BLÁS ARCHIPELAGO, PANAMA

Panama probably isn't the first place that comes to mind when you think of the Caribbean, but this Central American nation has coral cays to rival anything in the Caymans or the Virgin Islands. Run as an autonomous province by the Kuna people, the San Blás Archipelago is a crescent of 365 tiny islands basking in the warm waters of the southern Caribbean. Forget luxury resorts – the only hotels are homestays in village houses and dinner is whatever the fishermen bring home in their canoes each evening.

Air Panama (www.flyairpanama.com) has regular flights to several San Blás islands, including the capital, El Porvenir.

✪ PENGHU ISLANDS, TAIWAN

If Taiwan is the *other* China, then the Penghu islands are the *other* Taiwan. Administered from Taipei, the 90 islands of the Penghu archipelago are famed – within Taiwan at least – for their glorious scenery and 'touching nostalgia', which translates to unspoiled traditional Taiwanese culture. Away from the capital, Makung, this is a land of ox-carts, fish-traps, stone-walled fields, basalt cliffs and temples dedicated to the sea goddess Matsu. If sun and sand are more your cup of *shochu*, the beaches and windsurfing are pretty impressive too.

From May to October, Penghu's beaches are a nesting ground for endangered green turtles – locals leave turtle-shaped offerings at temples as part of the Lantern Festival, 14 days after the New Year.

✪ BAY ISLANDS & HOG ISLANDS, HONDURAS

Forget *Pirates of the Caribbean* – the sand-dusted islands that float off the coast of Honduras are the real deal. In their heyday, the islands of Roatán, Utila and Guanaja were home to 5000 cutthroats, brigands and buccaneers, including the infamous Henry Morgan (aka Blackbeard). These days, the Bay Islands are better known for their beaches, diving and laid-back tropical vibe. You can turn the volume down ever further at the nearby Cayos Cochinos (Hog Islands) – 13 languorous coral cays and one secluded resort in a sea of brilliant blue.

The driftwood Plantation Beach Resort (www.plantationbeachresort.com) is the Hog Islands' only accommodation, but camping can be arranged on uninhabited islands.

GET BLOOD FROM A DRAGON'S BLOOD TREE (IF NOT A STONE) IN YEMEN

FRANCES LINZEE GORDON » LPI

✪ CON DAO ISLANDS, VIETNAM

Another prison-turned-paradise, the Con Dao islands were home to the most notorious penal colony in Indochina, and continued its grim work until the end of the Vietnam War. Now preserved as Con Dao National Park, the 16 islands are a natural wonderland of dense jungles, jade-coloured waters and white-sand beaches, home to dugongs, dolphins, turtles and spectacular coral reefs. For now, tourist developments on the islands are limited to a single dive shop and a handful of resorts in Con Son township.

Timing is everything with Con Dao – the islands are lashed by squalls from the west from June to September and squalls from the east from September to January.

✪ SSESE ISLANDS, UGANDA

Why would a landlocked African nation appear on a list of desert islands? Thank Lake Victoria. The Ssese Islands tick all the right boxes for an island paradise – golden beaches, whispering palm trees, exotic flora and fauna – they just happen to be in the middle of Africa's largest lake. Most of the 84 islands in the Ssese group are undeveloped, but a handful of resorts and beach camps grace the sands of Buggala, Bukasa and Banda. Aside from basking in the sun, the main activities are combing the jungle for exotic creatures and canoeing across the lake.

Boats run daily to Kalangala on Buggala island from Entebbe, Kasenyi and Bukakata on the mainland.

LAST
COLONIES

THE AGE OF EMPIRES MAY BE OVER, BUT THE MAP STILL HAS A
FEW PINK SPOTS WHERE THE SUN NEVER SETS. HERE'S OUR PICK
OF THE LAST COLONIAL OUTPOSTS.

01 RÉUNION

Ask someone from France for the definition of paradise, and there's a good chance they'll say Réunion. Despite being 9500km from France, the Indian Ocean island of Réunion is run as a French overseas department, giving it a similar status to Ardennes or the Dordogne. In fact, you can even make a national-rate phone call to Paris while standing under a palm tree in the capital, Saint-Denis. French holidaymakers flock here for the weather, the beaches, the surfing and diving, and the chance to trek across the lava flows of an active volcano (flip-flops not recommended).

The surf breaks around Saint-Leu perform best from May to October, but beware of 'les dents de la mer' – the island is notorious for shark attacks.

02 PITCAIRN ISLANDS

Fletcher Christian knew he was onto a good thing when he fled the mutiny on the *Bounty* for a life of freedom on the Pitcairn Islands. All the more ironic then that these four tiny dots in middle of the Pacific Ocean became a far-flung outpost of the British empire. Despite having no airport or harbour, the islands are still run as an overseas territory of the UK, home to 50 islanders descended from the original nine mutineers and their Tahitian wives.

The only way to reach the Pitcairn Islands is the MV Claymore II, which sails from the island of Mangareva in French Polynesia every Tuesday (see www.visitpitcairn.pn).

03 HAWAII

The elephant in the room as far as colonies go, Hawaii was seized from the Hawaiian queen Lili'uokalani in 1893, and never given back. Perhaps uniquely among former colonies, the people of Hawaii overwhelmingly voted to remain under the control of their colonial overlords in 1959, when the islands became the 50th American state. For the 6% who voted 'no', however, Hawaii remains an occupied territory. There is a vocal independence movement, opposed to both American influence and the presence of the British Union Jack on the Hawaiian flag.

The only island where Hawaiian is the main language, Ni'ihau can only be visited on special tours, with permission from the island's eccentric environmentalist owner, Keith Robinson.

GER » IMAGEBROKER

✪ THE FALKLANDS

With tensions rising between Britain and Argentina over the oilfields in the South Atlantic, this might not be the best time to visit the most southerly outpost of the British empire – another way to think of it is that this might be your last chance! Despite being closer to the South Pole than London, the Falkland Islands are unmistakably British, down to the floral teapots, red post boxes and fluttering Union Jacks. And away from the pocket-sized capital, Stanley, nature reigns supreme – this could almost be the Shetland Islands with penguins.

Because of the touchy politics, the only air routes to the Falklands are weekly Lan-Chile flights from Santiago, or special RAF flights from Brize Norton in Oxfordshire (see www.falklands.gov.fk).

✪ FRENCH GUIANA

The only South American country to adopt the euro, French Guiana is another of the curious *départements d'outre-mer* left over from the break-up of the French empire. While most of South America was divided between Spain and Portugal, the northeast coast became French Guiana, Dutch Guiana (now Suriname) and British Guiana (now Guyana). Still administered by the pen-pushers in Paris, French Guiana is a growing destination for ecotourism and space travel, thanks to 8 million hectares of virgin rainforest and the Guiana Space Centre at Kourou.

Try to time your visit to coincide with the Cayenne Carnaval – the streets of the capital fill with revellers every Sunday from early January until Mardi Gras (Shrove Tuesday).

LINDA CHING » LPI

✪ WESTERN SAHARA

Not all colonies are isolated atolls. The pancake-flat deserts of the Western Sahara officially belong to Morocco, which seized the territory and its population of half a million people from Spain in 1975. Locals have been fighting for independence ever since, but the Western Sahara still has a fledgling tourism industry. Every year, a handful of visitors travel to the dusty capital Laâyoune – a dead-ringer for

Mos Eisley spaceport – to see what North Africa looked like before the era of mass tourism.

If you travel overland to Laâyoune, be sure to avoid the unfortunately named Berm, a 2700km-long sand barrier encrusted with landmines.

✪ TOKELAU

New Zealand was one of the last great landmasses to be snapped up by

European colonial powers, so it's all the more surprising to discover that the Kiwis have a colony of their own, tucked away in the South Pacific. The tiny, sand-dusted atolls that make up Tokelau are as close to Hawaii as New Zealand, but the government in Wellington has been in charge since 1948. Tourist attractions include fine beaches, coral-filled lagoons and collecting coconuts – plus the thrill of being one of only 40 outsiders to visit the islands every year.

Visits to Tokelau must be arranged through the Tokelau Apia Liaison Office (www.tokelau-govt.info) in Samoa – a lone freighter runs to the atolls every two weeks and there is a single hotel, run by the schoolmaster on Nukunonu.

✪ MARTINIQUE & GUADELOUPE

Back in the days of galleons and buccaneers, everyone wanted a piece of the Caribbean – France just decided to not give its piece back. Along with neighbouring Guadeloupe, the sun-kissed island of Martinique is a tiny extension of the French mainland, marooned in the Caribbean Sea. Islanders speak French, obey French laws, vote in French elections and pay for their swordfish steaks and Ti'punch cocktails in euros. Apart from that, this is the typical Caribbean, complete with coconuts, Creoles and carnivals (just be sure to stand for 'La Marseillaise').

The seacat ferries run by L'Express des Iles (www.express-des-iles.com) hop-scotch between Martinique and Guad-eloupe, with stops in Dominica and St Lucia.

✪ GUAM

The Americans were late arrivals to the colonial game, but they made up for lost time in the 1890s, acquiring Cuba, the Philippines, American Samoa, Puerto Rico and Guam in the space of just four years. The largest island in Micronesia, Guam is still a distant outpost of the US today, and the islanders are US citizens, with the right to nominate – but not elect – American presidents. As well as swaying palm trees and traditional island culture, Guam is famous for its WWII battlefields, which attract military history buffs from the lands of the free and the rising sun.

Guam is an easy stopover on flights from Asia to America, but avoid August to November, when tropical storms barrel down 'Typhoon Alley', bombarding the island with 240km/h winds.

✪ GIBRALTAR

You don't have to travel to the ends of the earth to find relics of empire. Britain has a conveniently located colony just off the coast of Spain. Encompassing an area of a mere 6.5 sq km, this tiny enclave at the mouth of the Mediterranean is as British as bangers and mash, apart from the Barbary macaques and *cerveza* (beer). Adding to the appeal, it doesn't take a week on an ocean liner to reach Gibraltar – you can walk across the border from La Línea de la Concepción in Spain.

For beans on toast, fish and chips or a proper British pint, head to Star Bar (www.starbar.gi), Gibraltar's oldest pub.

BEST
UNDERWATER
EXPERIENCES

IF, LIKE HOMER SIMPSON OR THE LITTLE MERMAID, YOU'VE EVER DREAMED OF LIVING UNDER THE SEA, CONSIDER THE FOLLOWING AQUATIC EXPERIENCES.

01 DIVING WITH GREAT WHITES, GANSBAAI, SOUTH AFRICA

Everyone knows how the *Jaws* theme music goes. Diving with great white sharks is up there with base-jumping in the adrenaline top 10, and Gansbaai in the Southern Cape is the ideal place to swim with the big fish. Fortunately, there's an aluminium cage – or for the brave, a clear plastic tube – between you and the ocean's greatest killing machines. Numerous companies offer dives in Gansbaai's 'Shark Alley', but look for operators who invest their profits back into shark conservation.
The Shark Lady (www.sharklady.co.za), aka Kim Maclean, pioneered shark diving at Gansbaai; peak shark season runs from May to October.

02 GETTING MARRIED UNDERWATER IN TRANG, THAILAND

If you fancy making a splash on your wedding day, consider an underwater wedding at Trang in southern Thailand. Every Valentine's Day, dozens of couples don scuba tanks and descend to an altar 12m beneath the Andaman Sea for a full Thai wedding ceremony. Wedding dresses are de rigueur and even the marriage certificate is signed underwater; the ceremony ends with the happy couple releasing one million baby shrimps and a giant clam onto the reef to gain Buddhist merit. Of course, it's tricky saying 'I do' with a regulator in your mouth...
The Trang Underwater Wedding Ceremony (www.underwaterwedding.com) runs from 12 to 14 February every year, and brides and grooms must be certified open-water divers.

03 SLEEPING WITH THE FISHES IN FIJI

Travellers with plenty of cowrie shells to spare can swap a night under the stars for a night with the starfish at the sparkling new Poseidon Undersea Resort in the Fiji islands. Suites are housed in futuristic pods on the sea bed, covered by acrylic domes and linked to the surface by a high-speed elevator. There's even a private submarine that guests can pilot around the lagoon. It's all very James

Bond, and the prices would make a supervillain wince.

There's a long waiting list for rooms at Poseidon Undersea Resort (www. poseidonresorts.com). If you have to ask the cost, you probably can't afford it.

✪ THE ULTIMATE FISH SUPPER IN THE MALDIVES

Taking the heights of luxury to the depths of the ocean, the Conrad Rangali Maldives resort offers every imaginable indulgence, including an eatery at the bottom of the briny. Covered by a curving glass canopy, the Ithaa restaurant floats beneath a curtain of swirling tropical fish, 5m below the surface of the Indian Ocean. Stingrays, groupers and sharks are regular visitors – think of it as an aquarium where the fish get to watch you eat. If you can see past the obvious contradiction, the menu runs to spiced scallops, tuna sashimi and lobster fricassee.

Visit the Conrad Rangali Maldives (www. hilton.com) from December to March for peak underwater visibility.

✪ SWIMMING TO YOUR ROOM IN THE FLORIDA KEYS

The only hotel in the world where you have to scuba dive to reception, Jules'

JEFF ROTMAN » ALMY

HOLD YOUR NERVE WHILE A GREAT WHITE TRIES TO FIGURE OUT HOW TO GET ITS LUNCH OUT OF THE TIN – GANSBAAI, SOUTH AFRICA

Undersea Lodge is housed inside a converted marine laboratory off the coast of Key Largo. Just six people fit inside this futuristic space, which opens directly onto the sea bed through a pressure-balanced wet room. The compact quarters might deter the claustrophobic, but the sea-lab setting is very James Cameron's *The Abyss*. Rates include meals – delivered from the surface in waterproof containers – as well as unlimited tanks for dives in the lagoon.

Advance bookings are essential for the two bedrooms at Jules' Undersea Lodge (www.jul.com), and guests must be certified divers or take a special introductory dive course.

✪ SNORKELLING WITH WHALE SHARKS, NINGALOO REEF, AUSTRALIA

Swimming with sharks feels a lot less scary when the sharks in question don't eat meat. Whale sharks grow to more than 12m in length – as long as a double-decker bus – but these gentle giants live off a diet of microscopic plankton. Whale sharks spook easily and the ideal way to get close is with a mask, snorkel and fins, so the best place to swim with the world's biggest fish is Ningaloo Marine Park on the west coast of Australia. Numerous operators run shark-snorkelling tours from the town of Exmouth in Western Australia.

Whale sharks visit Ningaloo Reef between April and July – at other times, you'll have to make do with manta rays, turtles, dolphins and humpback whales.

✪ SUBMARINE COCKTAILS IN EILAT, ISRAEL

According to Jules Verne, Captain Nemo frowned on alcohol and anything else associated with the surface of the earth, but the Red Sea Star would still be his kind of bar. Nestling on the seabed off the coast of Eilat, this wacky watering hole offers the rare opportunity to sip a sea breeze cocktail at the bottom of the sea. Okay, so the decor – wobbly windows, starfish lanterns, jellyfish chairs – is as tacky as an octopus's tentacles, but you can't fault the views over a coral garden teeming with fish.

Before you jump into your swimming costume, the Red Sea Star (www.redseastar. com) is attached to dry land by a 70m pontoon.

✪ WRECK DIVING IN TRUK LAGOON, MICRONESIA

The world of wreck diving owes a lot to WWII – whole fleets of warships were sent down to Davy Jones at Coron in the Philippines and in Scapa Flow in Scotland. But nothing compares to wreck diving in the tiny state of Chuuk in Micronesia. The sandy seabed of this coral atoll forms an eerie graveyard for more than 300 Japanese battleships, freighters, submarines and aircraft, sunk in a single devastating American assault in February 1944. However, dive carefully – the wrecks still carry their original cargoes of tanks, ammunition, torpedoes, depth charges and mines.

Continental Micronesia (www.continental. com) flies from Guam to the tiny airstrip on Weno island four times a week.

CHRIS A CRUMLEY » ALAMY

✪ FRESHWATER FROLICS IN LAKE MALAWI

Landlocked Malawi might seem an unlikely destination for a dive trip, but Lake Malawi has hidden depths (ahem). One of the world's top spots for freshwater diving, this African Great Lake is home to at least 1500 species of tropical fish, but significantly, no crocodiles (for some reason, they stick to the rivers feeding the lake). On the southern lakeshore, Monkey Bay is a prime spot to learn to dive: for one thing, the 'pool' training takes place in the warm, current-free waters of the lake.

In the chilled-out traveller centre of Cape Maclear, Gecko Lounge (www.gecko lounge.net) scores highly for its lakeside terrace and boisterous party vibe.

✪ DISAPPEAR INTO A BLUE HOLE IN MEXICO

The polar opposite of open-water diving, sinkhole diving offers the eerie experience of dropping into the dark unknown. Hidden away in the jungles of Yucatán, Tamaulipas and Quintana Roo, Mexico's *cenotes* – from the Mayan word for 'sacred well' – plunge to dizzying depths. Divers have descended to 282m in the still, silent waters of Zacatón in Tamaulipas without ever reaching the bottom. Leave your fear of confined spaces at the surface – the average blue hole is a tangle of stalactites, stalagmites and winding limestone passages.

Tulum in Quintana Roo is the undisputed capital of cenote diving, but you'll need special certification for cave diving.

FIERIEST FOODS

FOODS HOT ENOUGH TO REPEL ELEPHANTS AND MAKE CHEFS WEAR GAS MASKS? JUST READING THIS LIST WILL HAVE YOU REACHING FOR THE RICE AND YOGHURT TO COOL YOUR MOUTH.

01 BHUT JOLOKIA

The Guinness Book of Records has certified the *bhut jolokia* – aka Naga Chilli or Ghost Chilli – as the hottest pepper on earth. No surprise really, considering locals in northeastern India, where the little devil grows, have long used it as an elephant repellent. For reference, the *bhut jolokia* is about 200 times hotter than a jalapeno – which surely must render it too scorching for human consumption? Hardly. It's a staple in several Indian curries and often shows up in American sports bars as a manly, mouth-searing chicken wing sauce.
Grow your own bhut jolokia with seeds from the renowned Chile Pepper Institute (www.chilepepperinstitute.org; US$6 per package) in New Mexico, USA.

02 THAI YAM

Thai dishes are among the world's spiciest, and *yam* (hot and tangy salad) is the Thais' most potent plateful. Lime juice provides the tang and chillies the heat as they splash over herbs and a choice of seafood, roasted vegies, noodles or meats. The hot pod often called into action for *yam* spicing is the *prík kêe nŏo*, aka mouse-dropping chilli or bird's eye chilli, the premier tongue-torcher in the Thai arsenal. Many restaurant owners think Westerners can't handle the blaze, so they omit the dishes from their English-language menus. The *yam* section typically is the longest on their Thai menus.
Learn to spice it up at the Chiang Mai Thai Cookery School (www.thaicookeryschool. com), with one- to five-day classes for both novices and pros.

03 SAMBAL

Indonesians, Malaysians and their neighbours are silly for sambal, a garlic-laced, wickedly hot chilli paste mostly used as a condiment. In Indonesia there are almost more sambal variations than there are islands – pastes use tamarind and mango leaves, green tomatoes and fried peanuts. *Sambal ulek* is the no-nonsense standard. It's chillies, chillies and more bird's eye chillies ground by mortar and pestle, with maybe a dash of salt. Spoon it onto your fried tempeh or roasted fish and let the crying commence. The region's heated love affair began in the 16th century when the Spaniards dropped off the chilli from the New World.

CHRIS MELLOR › LPI

For do-it-yourself sambals and more, check out 'Authentic Recipes from Indonesia' by Heinz Von Holzen, Lother Arsana and Wendy Hutton.

✪ PHAAL

Some say the surface of the sun is made of *phaal*. That's a little far-fetched, since *phaal* is a curry dish. But you get the point: it's flaming, as in the most flaming curry in existence. UK restaurants invented the recipe, and to make it the proper way requires at least 10 ground chillies, preferably the *bhut jolokia*, *habanero*, Scotch bonnet or other top-of-the-heat-scale variety. Tomato, ginger, fennel seeds and meat or tofu comprise the rest of the dish – not that you'll notice after the first bite firebombs your mouth.

Finish your phaal at New York City's Brick Lane Curry House (www.bricklanecurry house.com) and receive a free beer and P'hall of Fame membership.

✪ SICHUAN HOT POT

Here's how the shirt-soaking sweat begins: you sit down in one of the ubiquitous restaurants in Sichuan, China where you'll find a burner on every table. The waiter places down a large metal pot split down the centre. One side holds red-tinged oil swimming with chillies and Sichuan peppercorns, the other side a milder fish broth. The waiter cranks the propane. The broths bubble and gurgle, and you toss in raw meat and vegies to cook your feast. The chillies? Sure, they're hot. But the secret weapon is the peppercorns, known for their numbing effect. Which means you eat a lot of hot before realising it (though all that sweating is a clue).

Hot-pot restaurants burn on every corner in Sichuan's capital city Chengdu – see www.cnto.org/chengdu.asp; the website also has visa information.

✪ PERUVIAN CAU CAU

Peru wins the prize for serving up South America's most eye-watering cuisine. Thank the *aji amarillo*, a homegrown yellow chilli that ranks right up there on the heat index (for comparison purposes: it's hotter than a serrano pepper but kinder than a Thai pepper). While the *aji* shows up in numerous dishes, it typically flares brightest in *cau cau* stew. Sometimes *cau cau* mixes tripe and potatoes, sometimes seafood, but always in combination with the chilli, turmeric and mint. Potatoes and rice accompany the dish to mitigate its blistering bite.

Pica Peru Culinary Vacations (www. peruculinaryvacations.com) encourages travellers to taste, chop and snack on local food in Lima and further-flung towns.

✪ JAMAICAN JERK

Brash, unforgiving and smoky, jerk done right will blow your head off. The concept is simple – meat marinated with

THE TASTY THAI DISH OF *YAM* WILL PUT A BIG SMILE ON YOUR FACE, TOO

spices – but the atomic blast comes from the Scotch bonnet chillies that steep the chicken or pork for 12 to 24 hours, permeating every cell. The meat gets hot, hotter and nuclear until it hits the barbecue pit. Jamaicans developed the spicy blend, which also includes big doses of vinegar, lime juice and allspice, as a way to help preserve meat in the 18th century.

Some say jerk was invented at Boston Bay; stay in the ecotents at Great Huts (www.greathuts.com) and follow your nose to the barbecue pits.

✪ YUCATÁN HABANERO SALSA

The *habanero* chilli originated on Mexico's Yucatán Peninsula, and it's still grown there in a fiery rainbow that includes green, orange, red, pink, brown and white varieties. Until the *bhut jolokia* came along, the *habanero* was the bad boy to beat for heat. Its distinct, almost fruity flavour makes it a culinary favourite, and a bowl of *habanero* salsa (charred chillies swirled with garlic, lime juice, salt, tomato and onion) sits on most Yucatán tables, to be dribbled – sparingly! – on whatever corn, chicken or fish dish comes out of the kitchen.

Visit organic growers, street vendors and local markets with Los Dos Cooking School (www.los-dos.com) in Mérida in Yucatán.

✪ WEST AFRICAN PEPPER SOUP

Ghana, Liberia, Sierra Leone and Nigeria all have their own versions of this West African staple. Although other ingredients may change – perhaps a chicken foot, maybe tripe, sometimes fish, often tomatoes – red peppers provide the common thread. The heat level can ratchet up rather quickly, especially when Scotch bonnet chillies are used, so cooks serve white rice or *fufu* (pounded yam dough) alongside to take the edge off. Medicinal bonus: French Army officer L Stevenel wrote in the *Bulletin of the Society of Exotic Pathology* in 1956 that the locals' lack of haemorrhoids was due to their red-chilli-rich diet.

With forts, beaches and jazzy highlife music, Ghana is an excellent place to begin a West Africa sojourn; check out www.touringghana.com.

✪ VINDALOO

Another Indian curry makes the list, though it's not quite as incendiary as *phaal*. The Portuguese introduced vindaloo to India when they sailed to Goa in the 16th century, and the name stems from the Portuguese words *vinho* (wine) and *alhos* (garlic), the original main ingredients. The Goans curried it up by adding mint, ginger, cloves and heaps of chillies, and the dish exploded over its meaty base (commonly pork or shrimp). Your tongue may throb in peppered pain, but remember this: chillies unleash endorphins in the brain, much like morphine does. That hot-spice buzz is the real deal.

Go to the source on a spice plantation tour in Goa (www.goa-tourism.com); November to March is the prime time for a visit.

THE GREATEST
COMEBACK CITIES

ONCE DEEP DOWN IN THE URBAN DUMPS, THESE CITIES HAVE BOUNCED BACK FROM THE BRINK OF BECOMING NO-GO DESTINATIONS, TURNING TUMULTUOUS PASTS INTO TOURIST DRAWCARDS.

01 BERLIN, GERMANY

Stalinist-style buildings were slated by contemporaries even as they were erected in post-WWII Berlin; architecture on Karl-Marx-Allee was mockingly dubbed 'wedding-cake style'. No surprises that now communism is kaput, Soviet-era hallmarks have been preserved with a degree of tongue-in-cheek. Preservation wasn't easy: following the Fall many favoured obliterating communist architecture. Now if Soviet sights are your thing you can, besides visiting the Wall, catch live music at the old Träenenpalast ('hall of tears'; where families said farewells near the Wall), see a movie at communist cinema Kino International or experience the DDR Museum, where exhibits even allow you to get spied on by the Stasi.

Soon after pre-Fall film 'The Lives of Others' was released in 2006, Ostel, self-styled 'Der DDR design hotel' opened its doors. Secure a stay in its communist-themed rooms by visiting www.ostel.de.

02 AYACUCHO, PERU

Now it's a colonial gem of the Andes rivalling Cuzco for majesty; 20 years ago it was the heart of the Shining Path terrorist movement that decimated the Peruvian highlands, with travellers steering well clear. The turnaround in Ayacucho has been monumental: paved roads only reached here in 1999. Since then tatty house facades have been spruced up and streets pedestrianised to get that idyllic, untouched-by-time feeling flowing again through the city. A cluster of chic-but-cheap hotels and restaurants have opened too, all in complete harmony with the buzzing colonial vibe.

Cream of the crop of charismatic colonial accommodation in Ayacucho is Hotel Santa Rosa. Check their Spanish-language website (www.hotel-santarosa.com) or call in (Lima 166, Ayacucho).

03 BEIRUT, LEBANON

Rallying from devastation is typical of Beirut: a city set back by two major conflicts in the last 30 years. Still, incredibly, meze and macchiatos are served up from its relaxed restaurants and cafes in a downtown rebuilt to its former grandeur. Hamra, a hotbed of Lebanon's civil war, now has shops and clubs favoured by an international following of fashionistas and partygoers. Formerly on the front line, Beirut National Museum was torn apart by militia fighting: renovation has seen the museum regain its status as a world-famous cultural centre. Much like the city as a whole, actually.

At the heart of downtown, Etoile Suites (www.etoilesuites.com) has individually designed rooms and a rooftop terrace.

✪ ASMARA, ERITREA

Many who have glimpsed visually arresting Asmara call it Africa's most beautiful city due to its innovative art deco architecture, built by Mussolini during his unsuccessful campaign to create a second Roman empire. For much of the last 50 years, however, Eritrea was embroiled in war with neighbouring

Ethiopia, first for independence and then over territory. Tensions between the countries remain, but the Eritrean capital is no longer off-limits. Its treasure trove of beautiful buildings now beg for discovery, including Benito's old party headquarters and Fiat Tagliero, a futuristic fuel station shaped like a plane poised for take-off.

Few hotels in Asmara have their own websites: instead visit www.asmera.nl for intriguing information on the city covering accommodation to architecture.

✪ GLASGOW, SCOTLAND

When the 'Glasgow's miles better' campaign launched in 1983, the city was being mentioned in the same breath as 'knife crime' and 'decay'. Campaign slogans, most famously fixed to rusting

RUSSELL MOUNTFORD » LPI

GERMANY AIMS FOR TRANSPARENCY IN GOVERNMENT WITH ITS PARLIAMENT'S GLASS DOME – REICHSTAG, BERLIN

gasworks in the industrial outskirts, initially seemed far-fetched: yet they worked. Glasgow reinvented itself and was soon winning accolades like European City of Culture. Championing industrial heritage became integral to new-look Glasgow. The once-grim River Clyde, heart of the city's post-WWII slump, has morphed into its cultural focal point with museums replacing derelict docklands. Ambling today through a centre of astounding architecture and cool cafe-bars, it's hard to imagine the bad times ever existed.

Trundle down the Clyde in the spirit of Glasgow's 19th century entrepreneurs on the Waverley, the world's last ocean-going paddle steamer (www.waverley excursions.co.uk).

✪ LEÓN, NICARAGUA

Beleaguered by earthquakes and blitzed during the Nicaraguan Revolution, it's a wonder León has emerged from the ashes of its all-too-recent past with anything left worth seeing, let alone oozing colonial charm. When it became the Revolution's first city to fall to Sandinistas, then-president Somoza famously responded: 'bomb everything that moves until it stops moving'. Plenty of signs from the conflict remain. Bullet holes from street fighting still riddle buildings; visit Museo de Tradiciones y Leyendas (Museum of Traditions and Legends) for an overview of the Sandinista rise to power.

Volunteer adventure group Quetzal-trekkers (www.quetzaltrekkers.com) runs volcano treks in the León region: profits go to help local street children.

✪ ROTTERDAM, THE NETHERLANDS

What is it about badly bombed cities and vibrant underground music scenes? Not that Rotterdam has nothing else besides its tradition of top electronica and hip hop to tempt travellers: its resurgence following the WWII annihilation of its historic heart has been remarkable. The area once blitzed has reinvented itself through cutting-edge design projects, recently including a series of colourful lights demarcating the limits of Luftwaffe bombardment. Blight took a while to become bite but cultural renaissance now pulsates through the 2007 City of Architecture, along with a feast of festivals celebrating everything from film to Caribbean carnival.

Dine out almost 100m up in Rotterdam's highest building, Euromast (www.euro mast.nl).

✪ VOLGOGRAD, RUSSIA

Sequestered in a portion of Russia rarely visited by foreign travellers, Volgograd and tourism have rarely gone hand in hand. Having seen Volgograd reduced to rubble after the Battle of Stalingrad (as it was formerly known), the then-US ambassador would lament this a 'dead city', but Volgograd is proving there is life after death. The battlefield is now renowned as an immense park of monuments to the Soviets that defended the city, crowned by the formidable 85m-tall Motherland Statue. Volgograd is a smart city but will never be a looker like St Petersburg – come instead for a moving crash course in WWII history at the many memorials and museums.

Aeroflot (www.aeroflot.ru) flies to Volgograd via Moscow; also consider S7 Airlines (www.s7.ru).

✪ YELLOWKNIFE, CANADA

Yellowknife rose to riches when gold was discovered nearby and slumped right back when gold-mining waned during the 1990s. Now the metropolis of Canada's Northwest Territories (population almost 20,000) has again put its dark days behind it. Thanks to a diamond boom the economy is as buoyant as a Hudson Bay seal pup and the town is reaping the benefits. Now a state-of-the-art heritage centre looks back fondly on the gold rush times. Meanwhile, in quirky Old Town (known as 'The Rock'), designer architecture is replacing the ramshackle huts of old; the wonderful Wildcat Cafe serves as a reminder of the tough gold-prospecting times gone by in Yellowknife.

Fish, kayak or go aurora-viewing on the lakes north of Yellowknife at homely Yellow Dog Lodge (www.yellowdoglodge.ca).

✪ BELGRADE, SERBIA

Ask anyone across the former Yugoslav nations: Belgrade is where the big night out is. Bombing during the Kosovo War along with one of the world's worst-ever hyperinflations brought the city to its knees but the music scene survived, booming to make this one of Eastern Europe's party capitals. Being the cradle of the 1980s Yugoslav New Wave got the ball rolling and Belgrade today is a music-lovers magnet. Repeatedly being razed to the ground also fashioned a riveting cityscape for Belgrade – a potpourri of ancient forts, neoclassic and modernist masterpieces. *Tune in to Belgrade's classical music extravaganza, Bemus Festival (www.bemus.org), or go wild up the road at Novi Sad's Exit Festival (www.exitfest.org).*

DIVE RIGHT INTO ALL OF THE ATTRACTIONS THAT BEIRUT HAS TO OFFER

10 BEST
THINGS TO CLIMB

OVER ICE AND IRON GIRDERS, SHINNYING UP TEMPLES AND
SCALING RAINFOREST TREES – TACKLE THE WORLD'S MOST
WORTHWHILE WAYS TO REACH THE TOP.

01 TIKAL, GUATEMALA

Ascending the steps of a 1250-year-old temple at the ancient Mayan megacity of Tikal to climb above the Petén jungle is one of Central America's greatest experiences. During the first millennium AD this site was the main metropolis of the Maya, one of the mightiest pre-Columbian civilisations. There are a clutch of ruins to roam, but tallest and most tantalising is Temple IV at the west of the complex. From the top Tikal's three other temples can be seen soaring out of the treetops – more unexcavated ruins lie hidden in the jungle.

Stay virtually on the edge of Tikal's temple-flanked central plaza at Jungle Lodge, with one of Petén's best pools (www.junglelodgetikal.com).

02 SOSSUSVLEI, NAMIBIA

The world's highest dunes, the world's oldest dunes... you won't be here long before the record-breaking sand statistics rear their heads, but Sossusvlei certainly boasts among the most mesmerising dunes on the planet for clambering over. Dunes here reach as high as 325m, but as sand walking is around 2½ times tougher than it would be on a normal surface, climbing is far from simple. The park Sossusvlei sits in, a swath of sand covering a good third of Namibia, fans out in all directions from the dune summits in a kaleidoscope of colours from blood red to amber to mauve. Stick to the dune's crests for the easiest ascents.

Dawn is ideal dune-viewing time: stay inside the park boundaries for those early starts at desert oasis Sossus Dune Lodge (www.nwr.com.na).

03 PERITO MORENO GLACIER, ARGENTINA

Hearteningly in these times of global warming, this glacier is among the few on the planet not actually retreating. Forming a 3km, 60m-high icy frontier against the lake it abuts, Perito Moreno advances only for lake water to periodically undermine and, in spectacular style, collapse it. Five-hour glacier treks bring you up close and personal to the glacier's myriad peaks, fissures and, if you're lucky, the ice cavern the lake hollows underneath, all effusing an ethereal blue glow. If the trek isn't a sufficient vertical challenge, try the ice climb, 20m up a sheer ice wall, and the ice abseil back down.

El Calafate is littered with agencies offering glacier tours. One of the best is Hielo & Aventura (www.hieloyaventura.com), Av Libertador 935.

✪ OLD MAN OF HOY, ORKNEY ISLANDS, SCOTLAND

Gather your grappling hooks, fasten your crampons – you'll need technical gear to scale this iconic sea stack, standing just offshore from some of Britain's highest cliffs on the wild island of Hoy. Flat, fertile Orkney isn't renowned for rock climbing but the Old Man is a big exception. The 450ft rock tower thwarted attempts to climb it until 1966, way after Everest had been conquered. Scale soon to avoid disappointment: one of the Old Man's 'legs' was washed away in 19th-century storms; geologists reckon the rest of the stack will ultimately follow suit.

Get detailed information on climbing Orkney sea stacks at www.ukclimbing.com. Guided ascents of the Old Man are possible: try http://northernskies.webs.com.

✪ VOLCANOES NATIONAL PARK, BIG ISLAND, HAWAII

Five volcanoes rise in a veritable smorgasbord of ruptured, frequently fiery peaks out of the lunar-like massif which makes up this World Heritage–listed

TODD LAWSON » LPI

WALK A FINE LINE AT THE SOSSUSVLEI SAND DUNES, NAMIBIA

national park: lava junkies should head here for a phenomenal fix. Not only are the world's most dramatic volcanic vistas located on Big Island (try the most active, highest and largest volcanoes) but the craters are easily accessible (a road runs round the rim of Kilauea). Roads shouldn't dishearten climbers from hitting the trails – some 240km of paths take the intrepid out to less-visited parts of the park. Check out offerings to Pele, Hawaiian Goddess of Fire, en route: gifts from seashells to gin are left to appease her fiery wrath.

Plan climbs and keep tabs on lava sightings in the park at www.nps.gov/havo. Drive in (US$10 per vehicle) or come car-less (US$5).

✪ CRAC DES CHEVALIERS, SYRIA

It's not particularly tough climbing this 12th-century Crusader castle but the challenge of ascent isn't everything, especially once you're greeted with the view from the parapets. Dubbed the 'most wholly admirable castle in the world' by TE Lawrence, the fortress stands atop a 650m outcrop on a historically important through-route to the Mediterranean coast. Crac was defensively sound enough for the Knights Hospitaller to make the castle their Crusade headquarters in 1142, and is famous for its walls never having been breached (despite multiple attempts by the Saracens). Reaching the battlements is easier for visitors today but the surrounding lush, ancient-monument-peppered Orontes Valley has changed little over the centuries. Scale early to avoid tour busloads.

Hama is the prettiest base for visiting Crac. Riad Hotel (www.syriaphotoguide. com/riadhotel) offers good-value city-centre accommodation.

✪ CANOPY WALKWAY, NEAR IQUITOS, PERU

For a long time this 500m walkway, strung between trees in the Peruvian jungle, was difficult to visit, with access largely restricted to researchers. It's easy to see why they flocked – this is one of the best ways to appreciate jungle birdlife on the planet. Now the intrepid traveller, too, can scramble up above the rainforest canopy to be put into prime viewing position for a visual feast of tropical avian activity.

Public walkway access is exclusive to guests of Explorama (www.explorama. com). Their ExplorNapo Lodge is a half-hour walk away.

✪ STOK KANGRI, INDIA

One of the world's only non-technical climbs in excess of 6000m, the peak of Stok Kangri often yields better views of the Great Himalayas than the Great Himalayas themselves. Allowing for acclimatisation, it's a four- or five-day trek to the summit. This is about as high as non-professional mountaineers get on the planet: a clear day sees exquisite views of K2, with the huge Ladakhi capital of Leh a mere speck on a horizon, hemmed in by the imposing mountains of the Karakoram Range.

Pamper yourself after your mountain exertions with a stay at the luxurious Grand Dragon Ladakh (www.thegranddragon ladakh.com).

✪ SYDNEY HARBOUR BRIDGE, AUSTRALIA

Ever seen Roger Moore's Bond in *A View to a Kill* and fancied climbing one of the world's largest bridges, girders and all? Your best bet lies in Sydney, not San Francisco, where scaling the Sydney Harbour Bridge takes you to a dizzying 134m above the photogenic harbour. Three types of climbs are offered on the planet's biggest steel arch bridge; wedding ceremonies have even been conducted on top. Vertigo-sufferers can content themselves with ascending the Pylon Lookout at the southeast end of the bridge: a modest 87m, climbed via steps rather than hair-raising catwalks.
Bridge-climbing is a popular activity in Sydney these days: visit www.bridge climb.com for details. The Pylon Lookout
(www.pylonlookout.com.au) is open from 10am to 5pm daily.

✪ MT KILIMANJARO, TANZANIA

Not featuring Africa's highest mountain in a compendium of great climbs, with its bird's-eye views of the wildlife-studded savannah way below, would be a travesty. At 5895m this clocks in as the highest freestanding mountain in the world, with a stunning variety of routes to the summit. One way up sees you accompanied part-way by a ranger to protect you against Big Game; others take you past Kilimanjaro's glaciers and have you camping overnight in a volcanic crater.
Climb above the Serengeti savannah without donning hiking boots on a safari by balloon (www.balloonsafaris.com).

DOUGLAS STEAKLEY » LPI

GO ICE CLIMBING OR JUST CHILL OUT AT THE PERITO MORENO GLACIER IN ARGENTINA

TOP 10 CITIES
FOR ARTISTIC INSPIRATION

THE CITIES WHERE HISTORY'S BEST ARTISTIC TALENTS HAD THEIR IMAGINATION FIRED – AND LEFT A LEGACY OF THEIR INSPIRATION BEHIND.

01 EDINBURGH, SCOTLAND

Scotland's literary output is phenomenal and most of its notable writers have been influenced by the capital. Famous resident Robert Louis Stevenson enthused that Edinburgh was 'what Paris ought to be'. Off the Royal Mile, the Writers Museum presents a personal side to the lives of Scotland's authors: exhibits include Robert Burns' writing desk. City writers had fingers in other bowls besides the inkwell however: Sir Walter Scott even helped rediscover Edinburgh Castle's Crown Jewels. Native artist Harry Raeburn preferred the city to both London and Rome: his *The Reverend Robert Walker Skating on Duddingston Loch* is one of Scotland's most iconic artworks. More recently, JK Rowling spent time in cafes such as the Elephant House drafting tales about a certain boy magician.

Drop into bizarre Surgeons' Hall Museum (www.rcsed.ac.uk) and discover Arthur Conan Doyle's inspiration for Sherlock Holmes, among other medical oddities.

02 ST PETERSBURG, RUSSIA

If street names sound familiar on your first visit to St Petersburg, it's because they feature so heavily in Russian novels. Gogol, Dostoevsky and Turgenev all lived along grand thoroughfare Nevsky Prospekt and the city's heart was frequently at the core of their work. There are more literary museums here than you can shake a ballpoint at, from the house of Pushkin (whose writing tackled the snobby superficiality of the St Petersburg wealthy) through to the digs of Dostoevsky (whose novel *Crime and Punishment* contrastingly focused on the city's deprived).

Continue jaunting through literary history at the Nabokov Museum (www.nabokov museum.org), the writer's birthplace and subject of several of his books.

03 BUENOS AIRES, ARGENTINA

It's easy to tap into BA's surging literary vibe: mainly because it's so cheap to while away hours in

JEAN-PIERRE LESCOURRET » LPI

the elegant cafes where the city's best writers hung (and still hang) out. The San Telmo and Palermo coffeehouses are ideal for espresso-sipping with the artsy in-crowd today whilst the city centre's glam Café Tortoni was formerly frequented by famed Argentinean author Jorge Luis Borges. Borges' house lies in Recoleta; his fictional *El Aleph*, the spot encompassing all other points in the universe, is supposedly located on San Telmo's Juan de Garay St. Finish your literary tour at Palermo's Garden of the Poets, bursting with writerly busts from Borges to Dante.

Treat yourself to San Telmo's tango-themed Mansion Dandi Royal Hotel (www.mansiondandiroyal.com), and learn

Argentina's national dance at the attached Tango Academy.

✪ VALPARAÍSO, CHILE

Chilean poet Pablo Neruda arguably did more than any other poet to preserve his country in words and Valparaíso, his home for many years, inspired him to plenty. He even dedicated a poem to his La Sebastiana house here, now a museum to the poet's life. Valparaíso is a visual stunner and others too have been moved to make art by its colourful twisting alleyways. Novelist Isabel Allende has set fiction here whilst cartoonist Renzo Pecchenino (aka Lukas) adored the cityscape so much he recommended every aspiring architect should study there. Valparaíso has a museum devoted to his works (www.lukas.cl).

Gran Hotel Gervasoni (www.hotelgervasoni.com) is a throwback to Neruda's Valparaíso: full of haughty period furnishings and perched high up in the city's hills.

✪ MUMBAI, INDIA

Being Bollywood's capital hasn't deviated Mumbai's sizzling cultural scene from its strong literary traditions and legacy of cutting-edge art. The city's love affair with literature dates back some way: in 1804 Scottish historian James Mackintosh founded the Literary Society of Bombay, now located in the neoclassical Town Hall. Renowned writers reared here include Salman Rushdie: his *Midnight's Children* is partly set in Mumbai. Ever since Independence

the city has nurtured India's most important art movements: savour Fort and Colaba district's snazzy galleries, featuring the country's most prominent artists.

Gallery Chemould (www.gallerychemould.com) has long showcased top contemporary talent including the Progressive Arts Movement, which shaped modern Indian artistic identity.

✪ HAVANA, CUBA

Without mentioning all that jazz, Cuba's capital has been a big artistic draw. The American author Ernest Hemingway spent much of his later life in Havana. His former home here is now a museum – even the gin bottles used to make his cocktails are on display. Track the writer's drinking trail to La Bodeguita del Medio, the bar where Hemingway liked to take his *mojitos.* Graham Greene visited Havana both before and after Castro's takeover – his spy thriller *Our Man in Havana* is partly based on experiences there.

Check into Graham Greene's favoured Havana hotel, the ornate 130-year-old Hotel Inglaterra (www.hotelinglaterra-cuba.com).

✪ LONDON, ENGLAND

You could plot a long, long literary pilgrimage around London, a city immortalised by writers from Charles Dickens to John Betjeman. In Bloomsbury, check out the Charles Dickens Museum in the author's former dwellings; the Bloomsbury Group, including Virginia Woolf, later frequented the district. Make Marylebone your mecca for a detective fiction foray. Sherlock Holmes' fictional house is at 221B Baker St, with a museum to the sleuth nearby; up at Regent's Park, Wilkie Collins was inspired to write *The Woman in White* after witnessing a lady screaming from a balcony. Drink like the artistic greats in East London's riverside pubs: Whistler and Turner patronised Wapping's Prospect of Whitby whilst Dickens sang for his supper at The Grapes.

Start your literary pub crawl at The Prospect of Whitby (57 Wapping Wall); continue downriver to The Grapes (76 Narrow Street).

✪ SAN FRANCISCO, USA

Any self-respecting writerly romp in San Francisco should kick-start at City Lights Books. Owned by one-time Beatnik Lawrence Ferlinghetti, City Lights published Allan Ginsberg's then-radical *Howl* poem in 1956. San Francisco's famous Six Gallery reading later became the event which brought the Beat Generation into public consciousness. Ken Kesey was then too young to become a fully-fledged beatnik but during nightshifts at Menlo Park Veterans' Hospital he gleaned inspiration to pen *One Flew Over the Cuckoo's Nest*. Fittingly, given its colourful past, San Francisco also sports world-famous street art – visit the Mission District for some moving murals.

Maybe get a glimpse of Ferlinghetti himself whilst browsing at City Lights Books (www.citylights.com).

✪ PRAGUE, CZECH REPUBLIC

As you might expect in a country whose first president was a renowned playwright, the Czech capital is a literary hotspot. Franz Kafka is among Prague's most influential exports: don't look any further than the Kafka Museum to get to the crux of the writer's relationship with the city. The capital has spurned a bookstore's worth of authors besides, including Milan Kundera, who writes about Prague politics and love during the 1960s and 1970s. The best spot for smooching with today's top writerly talent? Try Tynska Literary Café – a favourite with Czech writers promoting work.

Get the low-down on Kafka's life and times in Prague at Kafka Museum (www.kafkamuseum.cz).

✪ MEXICO CITY, MEXICO

'The bottom of the road' exclaims Jack Kerouac of Mexico City in *On the Road* and for a bunch of beatniks, Mexico's main metropolis was the ultimate inspiration. The beatniks had riotous times here; not least in the Zona Rosa bar where William S Burroughs accidentally shot his wife in a William Tell–type stunt with a champagne glass. Artists Diego Rivera and Frida Kahlo lived in the capital, creating a clutch of attractions: start with Rivera's bright Aztec-influenced mural at the Museo de San Ildefonso, Kahlo's Coyoacán house, or Museo de Arte Moderno (Museum of Modern Art), with works by both.

Party with the city's chic at Zona Rosa's Bar Milán (Calle Milán 18).

BEST
VAMPIRE
SPOTTING LOCALES

THESE UNDEAD FOLK ARE ENORMOUSLY HOT IN FICTION RIGHT NOW – BUT WHERE CAN YOU GO TO LEARN MORE ABOUT THESE CREATURES OF THE NIGHT?

01 BRAN CASTLE, ROMANIA

There's nothing better than going to the source, and in the case of vampire lore that's Vlad Ţepeş, legendary ruler of Wallachia, now part of Romania. Ţepeş became the scourge of the Ottoman empire and was fond of impaling entire Turkish forces sent against him. His bloodthirsty reputation inspired Irish author Bram Stoker to use him as the model for Dracula, and thus a legend was born. Bran Castle, one of his strongholds, now houses a museum dedicated to Queen Marie of Romania. It has an impressive clifftop profile, looking like the quintessential location for a vampire movie.

Bran Castle Museum (www.brancastle museum.ro) is located in the town of Bran, in Braşov county, Romania, and is open from noon to 7pm Monday and 9am to 7pm Tuesday to Sunday. Entry is 12 lei (US$3.90).

02 VAMPIRE BATS, COSTA RICA

The vampire bat has become inseparable from the legend of the vampire. Apparently inspired by a newspaper article about these inhabitants of South America, Bram Stoker wove their blood-sucking habits into his novel and the rest is history (or at least, folklore). These small bats do feed on animals' blood but rarely suck on humans, though there have been reported attacks in recent years in Brazil and Venezuela. One of the best places to see them in the wild is Costa Rica, especially within Santa Rosa National Park and Corcovado National Park.

Santa Rosa National Park in Costa Rica's north can be accessed via the Interamericana Hwy, or by regular buses from Liberia or La Cruz. At the other end of the country, southern Corcovado National Park can accessed by bus or car via the town of Puerto Jiménez.

03 MUSÉE DES VAMPIRES, FRANCE

Hidden away in the Les Lilas district of Paris is an enigmatic museum devoted to the vampire. Visits can only be made by appointment, but once through the forbidding red door, the visitor is treated to an eclectic collection of books, photographs, weapons, masks, models, costumes and other curios referencing the vampire legend. There's also a creepy Gothic garden out the back. *The Musée des Vampires (http://artclips. free.fr/musee_des_vampires/musee-homepage.html) is located at 14 Rue Jules David, Les Lilas. Visitors are welcome between 12.30pm and 8pm by prior reservation on +33 1 43 62 80 76.*

✪ FORKS, USA

When author Stephenie Meyer set her vampire novel *Twilight* in the small town of Forks, Washington, she had little idea of the wave of vampire tourism she was setting in motion. When *Twilight* went ballistic on the bookshelves, ardent fans headed for Forks, neatly arresting the slow economic decline caused by its traditional mainstay, the timber industry,

losing momentum. Now vampire fans can buy undead memorabilia, go on tours to locations that resemble Edward and Bella's literary hangouts, and celebrate Bella's birthday on 13 September. *Dazzled by Twilight (www.dazzledby twilight.com) offers three Twilight-themed tours of Forks and La Push, each priced at US$39/25 (adult/child).*

✪ VAMPIRE TOUR OF SAN FRANCISCO, USA

Anyone who's read Bram Stoker's *Dracula* will remember Mina Harker, whom Dracula attacked with the intent of transforming her into a vampire. Given that this curse was apparently lifted once he was destroyed, you might be surprised to find Mina Harker wafting about in 21st-century San Francisco, and sporting an American accent. But every weekend you can join

LUKE HUNTER » LPI

WATCH YOU DON'T GET BITTEN BY A BAT IN COSTA RICA – IT'D REALLY SUCK

Mina for a vampire tour of the city's historic Nob Hill. It covers documented San Francisco history as well as speculative supernatural events, and attendees are encouraged to dress spookily.

The Vampire Tour of San Francisco (www. sfvampiretour.com) commences at 8pm each Friday and Saturday from the corner of California and Taylor Sts, opposite Grace Cathedral. Bookings not necessary, tickets cost US$20 or US$15 concession.

✪ DRACULA TOUR OF LONDON, UK

Given the British capital's starring role in the original *Dracula* novel, it makes sense that there should be a vampire tour of its darker nooks and crannies. This supernatural outing takes in a house in Highgate where the vampiric one apparently lived during his London sojourn. It also takes in the ghosts of Highgate Cemetery, the satanists of Highgate Woods, and other dark denizens. Curiously, the whole thing is then followed with a medieval banquet. Blood, presumably, is not on the menu.

The Dracula Tour of London, run by Transylvania Live (www.dracula-tour.com), takes place nightly except Mondays, commencing at 6.30pm from Tower Gateway station on the Docklands Light Railway. It costs €109 (US$147); bookings essential via the website.

✪ PONTIANAK, INDONESIA

Vampiric creatures aren't just a Western obsession. Malaysia and Indonesia share the legend of the *pontianak*, supposedly the undead manifestation of a woman who has died during childbirth. This supernatural being is said to take the form of a beautiful woman, attracting men to their deaths by disembowelling them with her razor-sharp fingernails. You wouldn't really want to encounter one of these hellhounds, but if feeling brave you might visit the city of Pontianak, said to be named after the undead creature which once terrorised its men.

Pontianak is the capital of the Indonesia province of West Kalimantan, on the island of Borneo. Indonesia's national airline, Garuda (www.garuda-indonesia. com), operates regular flights from Jakarta to Pontianak.

✪ DRACULA'S HAUNTS, WHITBY, UK

Before Dracula reached London in the pages of Bram Stoker's novel, he came ashore at Whitby. The North Yorkshire seaport is famous for being the home base of 18th-century explorer Captain James Cook. However, no amount of historic circumstance can top Stoker's evocative description of the Russian schooner *Demeter* blown across Whitby's harbour with its dead captain lashed to the helm, crashing beneath the East Cliff before disgorging the vampire in the guise of a huge dog. As a result, Whitby has become a popular destination for vampire-fanciers.

The Whitby Gothic Weekend (http://wgw. topmum.co.uk) is held twice-yearly, in April and October, and features concerts, markets and comedy nights.

✪ BUFFY LOCATIONS, USA

Buffy the Vampire Slayer gained vampires a big new TV audience in the 1990s. If you loved seeing Sarah Michelle Gellar stake scowly-faced evil vampires while finding time to fall in love with a reformed one then you might like to visit the locations in and around Los Angeles where the series was filmed. The series' exterior scenes at Sunnydale High School were in fact filmed at Torrance High School. Shots of the fictional University of California at Sunnydale were taken at the UCLA campus in Westwood, and at California State University in Northridge. And the vampire mansion once lived in by Angel, Spike and Drusilla is the Frank Lloyd Wright–designed Ennis House near Griffith Park.

You can find a comprehensive list of Buffy locations within the IMDb (www.imdb. com) entry for Buffy the Vampire Slayer.

✪ DRACULA'S CABARET RESTAURANT, AUSTRALIA

If all this blood and gloom is getting you down, there is a way to take a lighter view of the vampire phenomenon. On the edge of the city centre in Melbourne, Australia, is a theatre restaurant named after the greatest vampire of all. Opened in 1980, Dracula's serves a three-course meal with a generous helping of over-the-top cabaret, inspired by horror but with a comic delivery. It's a notoriously cheesy night out, but the place has won tourism awards and is a sure counterpoint to the grimness of the vampire mythos.

Dracula's Cabaret Restaurant (www. draculas.com.au) is located at 100 Victoria St, Carlton. Dinner and show from A$68 (US$63); bookings on +61 3 9347 3344.

BRENT WINEBRENNER » LPI

SPOOKY COTTAGE AT BRAN CASTLE, ROMANIA – A SITE WITH A BLOODY REPUTATION

TOP 10
HISTORICAL RE-ENACTMENTS

THERE'S NOTHING LIKE STANDING AT A HISTORIC SITE AND SEEING ITS HISTORY DRAMATICALLY RE-ENACTED, VIA A COLOURFUL FAIR OR A NOISY SIMULATED BATTLE.

01 BATTLE OF WATERLOO, BELGIUM

This climactic battle of the Napoleonic wars would have been famous even if Swedish supergroup ABBA hadn't used it as the theme for their Eurovision-winning song *Waterloo* in 1974. Fought on Sunday 18 June 1815 near the town of the same name in Belgium, it ended with the defeat of the French by the allied forces commanded by the British Duke of Wellington and the Prussian Gebhard von Blücher. Nearly two centuries later, the battle is re-enacted in June each year, a spectacular sight for onlookers.
The Waterloo Battlefield (www.waterloo1815.be) is at Route du Lion 315, 20 minutes' drive from Brussels. The regular Battlefield Tour costs €5.50 (US$7).

02 JIDAI MATSURI, JAPAN

One of three major festivals held in Kyoto each year, the Jidai Matsuri's most popular aspect is its historical re-enactment parade. This colourful procession includes figures dressed in authentic costumes from various eras of Japanese history, aptly reflecting Kyoto's former role as the imperial capital. The parade includes members dressed as samurai, soldiers, workers, villagers and members of the royal court.
Jidai Matsuri (www.jnto.go.jp) takes place on 22 October each year. The procession departs from Kyoto Imperial Palace at noon, progressing to the Heian Jingu Shrine.

03 INTI RAYMI, SAQSAYWAMÁN, PERU

Before the Spanish conquest of South America toppled the Inca empire, the Inti Raymi festival was one of its most important observances. Held annually on the winter solstice, it honoured the sun god. Inti Raymi fell out of observance in the 16th century, but since the 1940s has been re-enacted each year at the Inca ruins at Saqsaywamán, on the outskirts of Cuzco. High priests and nobles walk along streets strewn with flowers to an old fortress, where they enact ceremonies based on ancient Inca traditions.

FRANK CARTER » LPI

Inti Raymi (www.cusco.net/articulos/inti raymi.htm) takes place on 24 June each year, and is free to view.

✪ CIVIL WAR REMEMBRANCE, USA

The American Civil War tore the US apart in the 1860s, dividing the north from the south over issues of slavery and states' rights. It's so recent, historically speaking, that it can still be a controversial subject today – right down to how best the war should be commemorated. Each year during the Memorial Day weekend in late May, Greenfield Village in Michigan hosts a Civil War Remembrance weekend. Re-enactors dressed as soldiers from each side, civilians, musicians and presenters all bring to life this period of conflict.

Greenfield Village (www.thehenryford. org/village) is located at The Henry Ford, 20900 Oakwood Blvd, Dearborn. Adult entry is US$22.

✪ BATTLE OF HASTINGS, UK

This pivotal battle in 1066 deposed England's existing monarchy and brought Norman rule across the English Channel by way of William the Conqueror. As such, it changed England's course dramatically, making it the most-remembered armed conflict in British history. Every year at Battle Abbey in the aptly-named Battle, East Sussex, the Battle of Hastings is restaged, with thousands of participants and spectators from around the world.

RICHARD I'ANSON » LPI

In addition to the clash of arms, living history encampments recreate 11th-century life.

The battle re-enactment (www.english-heritage.org.uk) occurs on the weekend either before or after 14 October. Adult entry is £11 (US$17), phone +44 870 333 1181 for more details.

✪ SOVEREIGN HILL, AUSTRALIA

The most tumultuous period of Australia's colonial history was the goldrush era of the 1850s, when prospectors from around the world descended on the enormously rich goldfields of Ballarat, Victoria. The era lives on at Sovereign Hill, an outdoor museum, with an unsealed main street lined with replica shops and pubs, and diggings along a stream whose bed has been salted with gold dust. Costumed residents stroll the streets, with outbreaks of staged re-enactments from actors playing 19th-century soldiers, miners, businessman and the scandalous courtesan Lola Montez.

Sovereign Hill (www.sovereignhill.com.au) is located in Bradshaw St, Ballarat, and adult entry is A$41 (US$38). A daily train from Melbourne, the Goldrush Special, connects with a bus from Ballarat station to the site.

✪ SIEGE OF MALBORK, POLAND

In the Polish town of Malbork sits a huge red-brick castle that seems way out of proportion to the village below. This is Malbork Castle, which was once known as Marienburg. In medieval times it was the headquarters of the Teutonic Knights, Germanic warrior-monks who established an empire in this part of Central Europe. It's one of the largest castles in the world, and each July it hosts the Siege of Malbork, a recreation of the 15th-century siege of Marienburg by Polish forces. It's a lively three-day event with costumed soldiers on horseback, sound-and-light effects, night-time attacks and lots of big swords.

The Siege of Malbork (www.visitmalbork. pl) takes place in late July each year. Malbork is easily accessible by regular trains from Gdańsk (45 minutes).

✪ BRISTOL RENAISSANCE FAIRE, USA

It's nowhere near Bristol… it's not even in England… but this annual fair does a good job of imitating the British port in the year 1574. That was when Queen Elizabeth I paid her visit to Bristol, so the event faithfully recreates the look and feel of Renaissance England. There's a great deal of theatre involved, with actors roaming the streets in costume, speaking Elizabethan English, brandishing swords and interacting with visitors. There are also a lot of diverting shops and rides if you tire of the historically correct.

The Bristol Renaissance Faire (www.ren fair.com/bristol) takes place at 12550 120th Ave, Kenosha, Wisconsin, from 10am to 7pm on weekends between early July and early September each year. Adult entry is US$18.95.

✪ RAPSKA FJERA, CROATIA

St Christopher is well known for being the patron saint of travellers, but he's also the patron saint of the island of Rab, Croatia. Which is a good reason to travel all the way there to take part in this annual fair involving a big dose of historical re-enactment. First held in 1364, the celebrations have a long pedigree. As they did then, they still culminate in a crossbow tournament. Before that event, you can amuse yourself by taking in displays of traditional crafts, a recreation of a medieval household and a vibrant costume parade.

Rapska Fjera (www.rab-croatia.com/fjera/ efjera.htm) takes place annually from 25 to 27 July. Ferries from the mainland port of Jablanac head to Rab all year round.

✪ INTERNATIONAL LIVING HISTORY FAIR, UK

For some people, historical re-enactment is a casual spectator sport, something to pep up the visit to a historic location. For others, it's a lifestyle. Attend this annual re-enactors' market and be amazed at the breadth of the products on sale by historically-themed traders from across Europe, and by the skills of the artisans and craftworkers who create them. Many re-enactment societies also promote themselves at the fair. Could you too be seduced by the appeal of slipping on some chain-mail and stepping a few centuries back in time?

The International Living History Fair (www. livinghistoryfairs.com) is held in February and October each year at the Warwickshire Exhibition Centre in Leamington Spa. Adult entry is £3.50 ($US5.20).

INDEX

ACKNOWLEDGEMENTS

PUBLISHER Chris Rennie

ASSOCIATE PUBLISHER Ben Handicott

COMMISSIONING EDITOR &
PROJECT MANAGER Bridget Blair

DESIGNERS Samantha Curcio, James Hardy,
Jennifer Mullins

LAYOUT DESIGNER Margaret Jung

MANAGING EDITOR Liz Heynes

EDITORS Nigel Chin, Jeanette Wall

IMAGE RESEARCHER Aude Vauconsant

PRE-PRESS PRODUCTION Ryan Evans

PRINT PRODUCTION Graham Imeson, Yvonne Kirk

WRITTEN BY Brett Atkinson, James Bainbridge, Mark
Beales, Joe Bindloss, Lucy Burningham, Stuart
Butler, Jean-Bernard Carillet, Matthew D Firestone,
Bridget Gleeson, Tom Hall, Paula Hardy, Abigail
Hole, Catherine Le Nevez, Jessica Lee, Marika
McAdam, Carolyn McCarthy, Anja Mutić, Brandon
Presser, Helen Ranger, Miles Roddis, Dan Savery
Raz, Robert Reid, Tim Richards, Rowan Roebig,
Regis St Louis, Ryan Ver Berkmoes, Luke Waterson,
Karla Zimmerman

THANKS TO Jim Hsu, Carol Jackson, Charity
Mackinnon, Kate Morgan, Carlos Solarte, Tony
Wheeler

LONELY PLANET'S
BEST IN TRAVEL 2011

LONELY PLANET'S BEST IN TRAVEL 2011
October 2010

PUBLISHED BY
Lonely Planet Publications Pty Ltd
ABN 36 005 607 983
90 Maribyrnong St, Footscray,
Victoria, 3011, Australia

www.lonelyplanet.com

Printed by Toppan Security Printing Pte. Ltd.
Printed in Singapore
Lonely Planet's preferred image source is
Lonely Planet Images (LPI).
www.lonelyplanetimages.com
ISBN 978 1 74220 090 3

LONELY PLANET OFFICES

AUSTRALIA Locked Bag 1, Footscray, Victoria, 3011
Phone 03 8379 8000 Fax 03 8379 8111
Email talk2us@lonelyplanet.com.au
USA 150 Linden St, Oakland, CA 94607
Phone 510 250 6400 Toll free 800 275 8555
Fax 510 893 8572
Email info@lonelyplanet.com
UK 2nd Floor, 186 City Rd, London, ECV1 2NT
Phone 020 7106 2100 Fax 020 7106 2101
Email go@lonelyplanet.co.uk

FRONT COVER IMAGE Steve Kelley/Getty Images TITLE PAGE IMAGE Dallas Stribley/LPI CONTENTS PAGE IMAGE Douglas Steakley/L
PAGE 7 IMAGE Jean-Bernard Carillet/LPI PAGE 207 IMAGE Margie Politzer/LPI INSIDE BACK COVER IMAGE Margie Politzer/LPI

LONELY PLANET'S
BEST IN TRAVEL PLANNER 2011

JANUARY

GRAND SUMO TOURNAMENT » TOKYO, JAPAN
Tokyo's Grand Sumo Tournament, an annual event as huge as its competitors, is a multiday battle between the sport's largest and most celebrated behemoths (p48).

PANAMA JAZZ FESTIVAL » PANAMA CITY, PANAMA
In mid-January, the Panama Jazz Festival draws international artists to jam in Casco Viejo's open-air plaza; the main event is free for spectators (p24).

UP HELLY AA » SHETLAND ISLANDS, SCOTLAND
This spectacular torchlit parade celebrates islanders' Norse heritage. Locals dress as Vikings and carry blazing torches; they parade a longboat through the streets before setting it alight (p75).

FEBRUARY

MANDI SAFAR » GILI ISLANDS, INDONESIA
At the end of the second month of the Islamic calendar (around 2 February 2011), locals venture down to the beach for a ritual cleansing ceremony that includes a dip in the sea, drumming, readings and the releasing of mango leaves bearing prayers into the waves (p91).

CARNIVAL » VENICE, ITALY
Carnival is celebrated all over Italy, most famously and fabulously in Venice, but you'll find fancy dress, parties, confetti throwing and celebratory sweets all over the country (p37).

CRICKET WORLD CUP » INDIA, SRI LANKA & BANGLADESH
The 2011 ICC Cricket World Cup takes place in February and March, hosted by India, Sri Lanka and Bangladesh, with 14 international cricket teams competing in a series of One Day Internationals. Watch India go even more cricket-crazy than ever (p125).